BEE

BEEKEEPING

BUSINESS STRAT UP

How to Start, Run & Grow a Million Dollar

ORGANIC HONEY

Business From Home!

By

Eddie Fisher

Published by:

Valley Of Joy Publishing Press
P.O. Box 966
Semmes, Alabama 36575

Cover & Interior designed.

Bye

Rebecca Floyd

First Edition

CONTENTS

THE BENEFITS OF BEEKEEPING

When I first heard about people starting to beekeeping in their backyards, I immediately thought, who needs that much honey? Then, I talked to a neighbor who got into it and realized there is much more to beekeeping than simply gathering honey. For one, I now know more about agriculture and the value of bee pollination. Several commercial crops would suffer without bee pollination. Even in a small backyard garden, there are dramatic improvements with bees: more yields and bigger crop production.

Certainly, one of the main reasons most people start beekeeping is the ability to harvest real honey. There is something unique about being able to bottle your honey. My first question was how much money you could get from your beehives. The answer depends on your beehives' weather, rainfall, and location. It is easy for a single colony to quickly produce 30 to 60 pounds of honey.

While honey and pollination are two excellent reasons for beekeeping, saving bees is also valuable. There are many areas worldwide where wild honeybees are becoming extinct due to urbanization, pesticides, parasitic mites, and Colony Collapse Disorder (CCD). All these things have devastated the honeybee population, and caring for a colony in your backyard can help save the bee population and give you the best pure raw honey for you and your whole family.

In this book, I'm going to talk to you not only about how you can start a beekeeping operation in your backyard but also how you can benefit from your hive. We'll look in depth at the benefits of having a beehive and how you can turn your excess production into a thriving business. I certainly have. Let's first look at the art of beekeeping itself.

TYPES OF BEEHIVES

If you've decided to get started with backyard beekeeping, you first need to determine what kind of beehive you want to build. For the bees themselves, the requirements are simple. A bee only needs four things from their hive:

1. A dark cavity
2. About 10 gallons in size
3. A dry location
4. A small entrance they can defend.

As a beekeeper, you will want a little more from your beehive. You will wish to a hive that is easy to work with, can be expanded in size, generates maximum honey production, and is easy to manage. It is essential to do some research before deciding on the best beehive for your needs. Let's look at some common beehive styles and their pros and cons so you can decide on the best beehive for your needs.

LANGSTROTH HIVES

This is the most common type of beehive. If you ever drive by a field and see a stack of white boxes with bees flying around, you know what a Langstroth hive looks like. Since these hives are so common, finding the material and equipment to start them is easy. The hives come in two different sizes: 8 frames and 10 frames. These hives were initially designed in 1852 by L.L. Langstroth. Most commercial beekeepers use these hives because they are convenient and produce excellent honey.

PROS

- ❖ Common and easy-to-find research materials.
- ❖ Eight frames are light and easy for beekeeping.
- ❖ It is easier for bees to move vertically to food in the winter.
- ❖ Everything is interchangeable since the equipment is the same size.
- ❖ Most bee supply stores stock supplies for these hives.
- ❖ The foundation keeps combs neat and in line with the frames.
- ❖ Can be built foundationless so the bee can have a more natural environment.
- ❖ Frames are less fragile in extractors than hives with no frame to support the comb.
- ❖ You can re-use frames of comb, which speeds up honey storage and population growth.
- ❖ Often has the most honey production of other hives.

- ❖ Ten frame hives are more expansive, and bees may not use honey on the edges in the winter.
- ❖ Needs more storage room when not in use.
- ❖ Inspections can be more invasive, letting more light and temperature change when opened.
- ❖ The foundation contains chemicals.
- ❖ When you reuse a comb, it will increase the chemical burden in the hive.
- ❖ If you build them foundationless, the bees can build across multiple frames and make the hive uninspectable.

KENYAN AND TANZANIAN TOP BAR HIVES

These beehives were first designed in ancient Greece, but today, they are very popular in East Africa since they are simple and cheap to build. They feature a horizontal cavity that allows the bees to attach their comb directly to the roof made from top bars or strips of wood. Above these top bars is a cover to keep out the elements. The horizontal design makes it convenient for beekeepers to open the back of the hive, smoke the bees to the front, and collect the honey from more aggressive bee species. The difference is that the Kenyan hives have sloped sides while the Tanzanian hives have straight sides.

Pros

* ❖ Inspections are less invasive, meaning less stress for the bees.
* ❖ If you build the hive yourself, they are much cheaper than other hives.
* ❖ Has fewer pests.
* ❖ Less lifting involved for those with handicaps.

- ❖ You can frequently harvest small amounts of honey.
- ❖ Bees can build a more natural cell size.
- ❖ There is little equipment that you need to store.

Cons

- ❖ More challenging to find support for these hives.
- ❖ It is easier to damage a comb since no framework supports it.
- ❖ When new packages of bees are installed, there is a higher rate of bees leaving the hive.
- ❖ More challenging to overwinter.
- ❖ Produces less honey than other hives.
- ❖ More time and resources are needed for the bees to build more combs.
- ❖ More visits are required to keep the new camp growing and aligned with the top bars.
- ❖ More challenging to treat mites.
- ❖ More difficult to feed in the winter.

WARRE HIVES

This is another beehive style that is gaining

popularity. It was first designed in France in the 1940s by Abbe Emile Warre. These hives are supposed to mimic a tree, which allows bees to attach the comb to the top bars in each box and extend them towards the ground.

As the hives fill, new boxes are added underneath, opposite the Langstroth hive system. Of the other two hives, this option is the most hands-off and requires the least support and research. The aim of these hives is to have light, inexpensive ones that are available to everyone.

❖ The 12-inch diameter is closer to a natural tree hive.

❖ When you build your own, they are the cheapest option.

❖ All boxes are the same size, making them interchangeable.

❖ It doesn't require inspections as frequently as other hives.

❖ There is no foundation, so they are more natural, with fewer chemicals.

❖ A quilt box will absorb moisture to reduce problems in both winter and summer.

❖ Bees are built down, which is a natural state for them.

❖ When you remove a box of honey, you remove the oldest, which helps keep your hive from getting contaminated.

❖ There is less equipment involved.

❖ The boxes are lighter than a Langstroth hive.

CONS

- ❖ More challenging to find information and support.
- ❖ It is more complicated to build than the top bar hives.
- ❖ It can be heavy to put empty boxes under full ones when expanding your hive in the spring.
- ❖ You may need to purchase a hive lift.
- ❖ More difficult for bees to cluster and travel in the winter in northern climates.
- ❖ Special handling needs to be learned since the combs are more fragile.
- ❖ More challenging to treat mites.
- ❖ more complex to assess through an observation window when compared to inspections in other hives.
- ❖ Lifting these boxes can be heavy.
- ❖ Honey yields are lower with these hives than others.

These are just the three most common types of beehives. There are plenty of other options out there as well. With some research and trial and error, you can find a beehive option that works best for you and your location. As you can see, they each come with various pros and cons that you need to consider. Let's take the first type of hive we've discussed and see how you can build your hive.

I started with Langstroth Hives, as it is the easiest and time-tested than all others.

BUILDING A BEEHIVE

When it comes to beekeeping, it is essential to determine the type of hive you want and build it so your bees have someplace to live when you bring them home. The most common beehive is the Langstroth hive (which is why I went with this kind), so let's look at how to build these hives. First, you want to consider the parts of the hive.

PARTS OF THE LANGSTROTH HIVE

➢ Outer/Telescoping Cover—This cover maintains a dry hive during rain and functions like a house's roof.

➢ Inner Cover—This cover contains a bee escape, which is valuable for collecting honey. This board is placed below the honey superb, which causes the worker bees to move into the brooding chamber but prevents them from moving towards you.

➢ Shallow/Honey Super - This is the location where honey is stored.

➢ Queen Excluder - This is a pass-through for the

worker bees and keeps the queen and drones away from the honey.

➤ Frames - The place where the honeycomb is created so you can collect honey.

➤ Foundation - This artificial comb will encourage the bees to produce more honeycomb.

➤ Brood Chamber - The location where queens and drones give birth.

➤ Entrance Cleat - The entrance to the hive for bees in the winter.

➤ Bottom Board - What do you place the hive upon? This reversible bottom board has two rims: a short one for winter and a tall one for summer.

➤ Hive Stand - Keeps your hive off the ground to prevent it from rotting.

When constructing a beehive, there are a few goals to remember. You want to make sure your hive meets the following requirements:

✓ Shelter from the wind.
✓ Located above stagnant water.
✓ It can be warmed by the morning sun.
✓ Located near a water source.
✓ Painted according to your region without toxic

paints. For example, white is often used to reflect the sun's heat.

✓ Protected by a barrier from objects and people that can cause the bees to be a nuisance and/or the bees can be injured.

It is also vital that you place your hives in suitable places.

WHERE TO LOCATE YOUR BEEHIVE

You can get started with backyard beekeeping anywhere since they don't require a large amount of space or a lot of specialized equipment. You don't need much food since bees will happily travel miles to get what they need. However, a few tips for placing your beehive can help you get a better honey harvest.

You want to ensure easy access to your hive so you can tend to it. It also needs to be in a location with good drainage to prevent your bees from getting wet. There should be a nearby source of water, intermittent sunlight, and not a lot of wind. It may not be possible to meet all these criteria when finding a location for your beehive, but you must do your best. The following are the things you can do to help you increase your chances of meeting all these criteria.

First, you can try facing your hive to the

southeast. This will help your bees wake up earlier and start foraging earlier.

The most important thing is to position your hive so that you can easily access it when you want to harvest honey. You don't want to be hauling hundreds of pounds of honey on a hot day during harvest.

You also want to provide a windbreak at the back of your hive. This can be in the form of trees, or a fence made from burlap. This barrier will help to block harsh winter winds that will cause stress to your colony, especially if you live in a colder climate in the winter.

For intermittent sunlight, you want to place your hive someplace that avoids full sun. Too much sun will cause the colony to work harder to regulate the hive temperature in the summer months. However, you also want to avoid deep, dark shade since this will cause the hive to become damp and lead to colony listlessness.

It is also important to ensure good ventilation

in the hive. You don't want to place your hive anywhere where the air is still and damp. You should also avoid locations on the peaks of hills because they will be bad in the winter months.

You want to make sure that your beehive is placed completely at a level from side to side. The front of the hive should be slightly lower than the rear, at a difference of about an inch or less. This allows rainwater to drain out of your hive rather than into it. Locating your hive on firm, dry land is also essential, so it doesn't sink into the dirt. Placing mulch around the hive will prevent grass and weeds from growing up and blocking the entrances.

If you ever need to move your hive to a new location, you will need to take extra precautions. When moving your hive, a mile or two, you have no problems because you are planning to start a new colony. However, when moving your hive for shorter distances, you risk losing your field bees since they will return to the old hive location.

If you move your hive a short distance, you want to do it a bit at a time, perhaps a few yards a day until you get it to the new location.

After getting your hive ready, it is time to research the bees you want to add to it.

CHOOSING THE RIGHT TYPE OF BEES FOR YOUR HIVE

Once you have a hive, your next big decision is to choose what types of bees you want in your hive. Growing up, we all have heard about honey bees, bumble bees and many other names and varieties. But first, let's understand that there are three types of bees under every category. There are worker bees; then there is the Queen and the Drones. These are the three that make up the colony. More on that later, but let's first talk about all the varieties you must choose from.

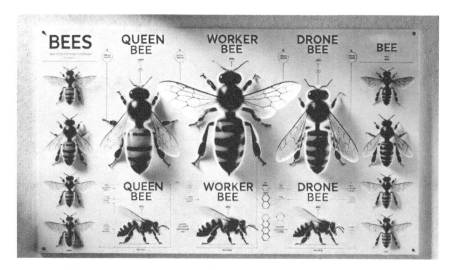

There are many different races of bees and hybrids of honeybees. Each strain of bees has its pros and cons that you need to consider. Let's look at the most common types of bees that you can quickly get from bee suppliers.

ITALIAN (A.M. LIGUSTICA)

These are yellow-brown types of honeybees with distinctive dark bands. They are good at producing combs and have a large brood that produces quick colony growth. However, they also have a large winter colony requiring a large food store.

CARNIOLAN (A.M. CARNICA)

These bees are dark in color and feature broad gray bands. They are known for their tendency to swarm. In the winter, they maintain a small colony that doesn't require much food.

CAUCASIAN (A.M. CAUCASICA)

These bees are primarily gray and adapt well to harsh weather conditions. The bees do well block drafty openings, which can challenge new beekeepers. Caucasian bees are also known for robbing honey, which can be a little chaotic for those new to beekeeping.

BUCKFAST (HYBRID)

Brother Adam, a Benedictine monk at Buckfast Abby in the United Kingdom, created this bee. It is known for rearing brood but can also rob and abscond from the hive.

RUSSIAN

Russian bees are adept at coping with parasites that have affected other strains of bees. However, they curtail brood production if pollen and nectar are in limited supply, so you will have a small winter colony.

Starline (Hybrid)

This bee comes from a combination of Italians and is the only commercially available hybrid Italian bee race. It is adept at pollinating clover and is sometimes called the Clove Bee. They look very similar to Italian bees.

Midnite (Hybrid)

Midnite bees are known for using propolis, making it difficult to inspect for the beginning beekeeper. The Midnight bee is a hybrid of the Caucasian and Carniolan bees. They look very similar to Caucasian bees.

Africanized (Hybrid)

This bee is the only one on this list that isn't commercially available, and I included it only as an example of a non-desirable bee. It is typically found throughout South America, Mexico, and some parts of the southern United States. These very aggressive bees make them difficult and dangerous to manage.

When choosing the right kind of bee for your hive, you want one that is gentle, produces well, tolerates diseases, and survives winter well, especially if you live in a cold climate such as the northern United States and Canada. For new beekeepers, it is best to try Italian or Russian bees since they are gentle, easy to care for, and do well in various climates. As you gain experience, you may choose to raise your species and hybrids of bees. To breed bees, you must take the time to learn about their biology, entomology, and genetics.

This is a totally different topic from what I sat here to discuss today. If any of you want to learn about breeding, maybe I can share that at a later time. But for now, let's just focus on where you can get some bees to start your hive.

WHERE TO GET BEES

If you're going to be a beekeeper, then you need bees. You must get some once you've built your hive and determine what type of bees you want. Let's consider where you can go to get your bees.

SOCIAL STRUCTURE

Before you buy some bees, it is essential to consider the social structure of a bee colony briefly. Bees are very social creatures, and a queen can't produce an entire colony alone. This is why you want to understand how a bee society works. A bee community has three levels: the worker, the drone, and the queen.

Worker bees are all females and perform various activities, including tending to the queen, building combs, guarding the entrance to the hive, and collecting food. The drones are all males; their only job is to mate with the queen, who passes on all the colony's genetic traits.

Bees in the Wild

You'll often see swarms of bees in the wild. Bees in the wild will divide a colony if reproducing too rapidly or if the queen becomes sick or injured. It isn't hard to collect a swarm of bees in the wild since they are often mild-mannered. However, you should still wear proper clothing and carry medicated syrup or a smoker when gathering bees in case there are ill-tempered bees.

You can also collect bees on tree limbs by cutting the limb and gently placing or shaking the limb inside a container. Bees on a flat surface can be guided into a container with a brush from cardboard. You can also direct bees by puffing smoke behind them, encouraging them to move in any direction. Then, you only need to transfer the bees from the container to your hive.

However, sometimes, getting your bees from the wild isn't the best option. Wild bees can have diseases or weak genetic material. You may have an injured or dead queen after the process. Also, it can be difficult to find wild bees. Lastly, some states have laws about what is considered property, and taking bees can be regarded as stealing. Before you try to catch wild bees, you should look into your local ordinances.

Purchasing Bees

Some professional beekeepers advise against purchasing bees since wild bees are adapted to natural diseases in the area. However, buying your bees is likely the most straightforward option if you are starting with beekeeping. You can purchase bees in two ways: packaged bees and nucleus. Let me explain both.

Packaged Bees

You'll need to contact a local beekeeper to get a package of bees. Most packages contain a queen, multiple workers, and a feeder with sugar syrup or other sweet food. You can introduce the queen bee to the worker directly or indirectly.

DIRECT METHOD

This option immediately releases the queen into the bees. Since most bees are packaged with a queen that isn't their own, there is a greater chance they'll attack the queen with this option. Without the queen, your hive wouldn't survive. However, if this method succeeds, you can start breeding immediately and produce honey quicker than with the indirect method.

INDIRECT METHOD

This option allows the worker bees time to become familiar with the queen. Place some food and give the worker bees time to eat their way to the queen.

You can also order a nucleus hive, which comes stocked with an established bee colony. The disadvantage is that the queen may be older or of poor stock, leading to weaker bees.

Having the appropriate equipment and tools to manage your bees is also essential. Let's consider what you should have on hand.

Depending on your location, a decent set of packaged bees, including the queen, may cost you around $100-$175. A typical package includes around three pounds of bees, enough to get you started.

Here is a YouTube video of how bees are packaged; look.

https://www.youtube.com/watch?v=AKWVq-bZ9Ok

BEEKEEPING TOOLS AND ACCESSORIES

There are plenty of tools and accessories targeted towards the backyard beekeeper. However, some of these supplies are more useful than others. Let's look at the essential tools and accessories you need for your beehive.

SMOKER

A smoker is a must for beekeepers. Smoke calms bees and allows you to inspect your hive safely. A smoker is a fire chamber with bellows that produce cool smoke. Finding a good smoker means finding one with the qualities below.

HIVE TOOL

This is a versatile and simple tool. It can scrape wax and propolis off wooden hives, loosen hive parts, open the hive, and manipulate the frames. Various models are available, so you are sure to find one that is easy to operate.

VEILS

You must always wear a veil when approaching a beehive. While your new beehive is likely filled with gentle bees, especially during the first few weeks of a season, you don't want to place yourself at risk. As a colony grows and matures, you will go near about 60,000 bees.

While bees aren't aggressive, they are curious and like to explore dark holes, several of which are on your face. You will find a variety of veils in different price ranges. Some veils are simple, while others are attached to full jumpsuits. Find a style that appeals to you and is based on the aggressiveness of your colony. Consider having a simple veil or two on hand if you have visitors.

GLOVES

A lot of new beekeepers want to wear gloves. However, you should use gloves when installing new bees or during routine inspections. Gloves will only make it more challenging to work with your hive and can cause bees to be injured.

This can not only stress your bees but can also make them more defensive. However, this doesn't mean you don't need to purchase gloves. There are still a few times when having gloves is a good idea:

✧ Late in the season when a colony is the strongest.
✧ During honey harvesting, since bees are more protective.
✧ When moving a hive body.

ELEVATED HIVE STAND

You may choose to build rather than purchase this. The simplest stands are made from 14-inch lengths of two-by-fours and a single plank of plywood that can hold the hive. You can also use cinder blocks to elevate your hive off the ground.

FRAME REST

The rest of this frame hangs on the side of the hive. It provides a convenient and secure place to rest your frames during inspections. It will hold up to three frames, so you have plenty of room to work within the hive and manipulate other frames without harming the bees.

BEE BRUSH

A bee brush is designed with long, super-soft bristles that allow you to remove bees from frames and clothing without harming them. Some beekeepers choose to use goose feathers.

SLATTED RACK

It can be a good idea to add a slated rack between the bottom board of the hive and the lower deep-hive body. This will help with air circulation in the hive. It also prevents cold drafts from getting in front of the hive, which causes the queen to lay eggs right in front of the combs.

After you are prepared and have everything in place, you will want a beekeeping calendar to keep you on schedule when maintaining your hive.

DEVELOPING A
BEEKEEPING CALENDAR

Your beekeeping calendar will be different whether you are in Vermont or Texas. The dates and activities you do will vary depending on the weather conditions in your area. Consider the following to help you develop a good beekeeping calendar for your location. First, you need to determine what zone of the United States you live in so you can evaluate your calendar schedule.

ZONE A: This area has short summers and long, cold winters. The average annual temperature is between 35 and 45 degrees Fahrenheit, and the minimum temperatures are often between 0 and 15 degrees Fahrenheit.

ZONE B: Areas with hot summers and extended cold winters. The average annual temperature is between 45 and 55 degrees Fahrenheit. The minimum temperatures are often between 15 and 20 degrees Fahrenheit.

ZONE C: Areas with a long, hot summer and a mild, short winter. The average annual temperature is between 55 and 65 degrees Fahrenheit. The minimum temperatures are often between 30 and 35 degrees Fahrenheit.

ZONE D: These are areas that are warm to hot all year. The average annual temperature is between 65 and 80 degrees Fahrenheit, and the minimum temperatures are often between 30 and 40 degrees Fahrenheit.

Determine your zone and then use the table below to determine what activities you should do and when to set up a beekeeping calendar.

Activity	Jan	Feb	Mar	Apr	May	Jun
Check food reserves	B	B	A, C	A	A	
Feed colony if low on capped honey	B, D	B, D	A, B	A, B	A	

Check for eggs/queen		D	B, C	B, C	A	A
Reverse hive bodies			B	C	A	
Install new bees in the hive				B, C, D	A, B	
The first inspection of the season		C, D	C, B	B	A	
Check for capped brood and brood pattern		D	B	B, C	A, B, C	A, B
Feed a pollen substitute		C, D	A, B, C	A, B, C		
Look for swarm cells			D	B, D	A, B, C, D	A, B, C
Add queen excluder and honey				B, C, D	A, B, C, D	A, B, C,

supers						D
Check ventilation						D
Add mouse guard						
Medication for AFB, EFB, and Nosema	D	C	B	A		
Check surplus honey		D	D	D	A, B, D	A, B, C
Harvest honey				D	B, D	B, D
Test for varroa mites		C, D	B	A	D	
Medicate for varroa mites if needed		C, D	B	A	D	
Medication for tracheal mites		C, D	B	A		

Activity						
Check for small hive beetle and medicate if needed		C, D				
Prepare hive for winter						
Check entrance for blockage	A, B, C	A, B, C				
Order new bees	A, B, C, D					

Activity	Jul	Aug	Sep	Oct	Nov	Dec
Check food reserves	B	B		A, B, C, D		
Feed colony if low on capped honey	B	B	B	A, B, C, D	C, D	D
Check for eggs/queen			C	D		
Reverse						

hive bodies						
Install new bees in the hive						
The first inspection of the season						
Check for capped brood and brood pattern	A, B	B				
Feed a pollen substitute						
Look for swarm cells						
Add queen excluder and honey supers						
Check ventilation	B, C,	C, D	B	A	A	

	D					
Add mouse guard			B, C	A, B		
Medication for AFB, EFB, and Nosema		A, B	C, D			
Check surplus honey	A, B, C	A, B	C			
Harvest honey	B, D	B				
Test for varroa mites		A, B	A, D			
Medicate for varroa mites if needed		A, B	A, C, D			
Medication for tracheal mites		A, B	A, C, D			
Check for small hive			C, D			

beetle and treat if needed						
Prepare hive for winter			A, B	A, B, C	C	
Check entrance for blockage					A	A, B
Order new bees						

Flowers are an essential part of keeping bees. Let's look at some of the most important plants you can plant to help your bees have a thriving hive.

FLOWERS AND BEES

If you have a beehive, it stands to reason you'll also have flowers. Bees gather the nectar and pollen needed for plants to reproduce. The pollen also feeds baby bees, and the nectar becomes honey.

It is a complete cycle. While bees get pollen and nectar from several trees and shrubs, several flowers contribute to the development of bees and can get you a bumper crop of honey. Consider adding some flowers to your garden to improve your beehive. It is also important to note that each type of nectar will give your honey a unique flavor.

ASTERS

The Aster family includes nearly 100 different species of flowers. Aster is a common wildflower that comes in a variety of colors, from white to pink and light to dark.

They can range in height from six inches to four feet and are often bushy. They are primarily perennials and bloom anywhere from early spring to late fall.

SUNFLOWERS

Sunflowers come from two families: Helianthus and Tithonia. They provide pollen and nectar for bees. Sunflowers can be readily grown from seed; a few nurseries will carry them as potted plants.

If you start sunflowers early in the season, you want to make sure you use peat pots. Sunflowers proliferate and transplant best when you leave the roots undisturbed by planting the entire pot.

SALVIA

This family has over 500 varieties, including sages and many bedding plants. Sages provide good nectar; when they are in full bloom, you'll see they are covered with bees all day.

BEE BALM

This perennial herb provides a long-lasting flower in midsummer, either pink, red, or crimson. The flowers grow to about 8 inches before flowering and then grow to 3 or 4 feet tall.

You can encourage more growth by deadheading them. This plant is prone to powdery mildew, but the Panorama type doesn't have this problem as severely. In addition to providing nectar for bees, these plants also attract butterflies and hummingbirds.

HYSSOP

This plant has a licorice fragrance when the leaves are bruised. In midsummer, it grows tall spikes of purple flowers. Occasionally, you will find a white colored variety of this plant. This plant is also fast growing, often flowering from seed in the first year it is planted.

MINT

Several varieties are available, including chocolate, spearmint, apple, peppermint, and orange mint. You will find them in various colors, sizes, fragrances, and appearances. No matter what plant you have, the bees will come when the plant flowers.

Often, this plant blooms later in the year.

CLEOME/SPIDER FLOWER

This plant is heat- and drought-tolerant but doesn't do well in the cold Northeast. It is easy to start with a seed, and it grows up to four feet tall with large flowers that are six to eight inches across. It comes in white, pink, and light purple colors. It is an excellent option for those not adept at growing and blooms from midsummer to fall.

THYME

The various varieties of this plant are low-growing and hardy herbs; a few include standard, French, woolly, silver, and lemon. Most nurseries stock these plants in large amounts in spring, or you can start them from seed. In addition to providing food for your bees, you can also use the plants in your cooking.

POPPY

The three varieties of this plant that grow the best from seed are the Danish flag, corn poppy, and Iceland poppy. You will find them in deep scarlet and crimson colors and pastel varieties. The poppy blooms freely from early summer to fall and does best in full sun.

They grow up to two to four feet tall. The California poppy is very popular. Its golden orange flower provides a good pollen source for bees.

BACHELOR'S BUTTONS

This plant is available annually and perennially.

The annuals are available in white, pink, yellow, purple, and blue shades. Sometimes, this plant is also referred to as cornflowers.

The perennial version is often a shade of blue and grows in early summer and sometimes in late fall. Both plants offer a plentiful supply of nectar for your bees.

Keeping a beehive can be much work and requires individual tasks all year round. Consider what you must do each season to have a thriving hive.

Keeping a Beehive

While the seasonal calendar of beekeeping events will vary depending on your climate, there are still some general rules for caring for bees throughout the seasons.

No matter what, general seasonal changes impact their location. Knowing what significant activities are happening in the hive and what you are expected to do. So, let's look at what you must do during the four major seasons.

In the Summer

During summer, the nectar flow usually reaches its peak, and the colony population also reaches its peak. Currently, the colony is usually pretty self-sufficient, with the worker bees collecting pollen, gathering nectar, and making honey. However, during late summer, the queen also drops her rate of laying eggs.

It is important to note that on hot and humid nights, you'll see a curtain of bees on the exterior of your hive. If you notice this, you may consider adding more ventilation holes to provide your colony with better ventilation. This signifies that your bees are trying to cool off from the heat.

By late summer, colony growth begins to slow. The drones are still around, but outside activity slows as the nectar flow diminishes. At this time, the bees often become restless and more protective of their honey.

Summer To Do List

✓ Inspect the hive at least every other week to ensure it is healthy and the queen is still present.

✓ As needed, add honey supers.

✓ Through mid-summer, try to keep the colony swarm under control.

✓ Watch honey-robbing wasps or other bees.

✓ Harvest your honey crop at the end of the nectar

flow. If you are in a zone with cold winters, remember the colony will require at least sixty pounds of honey to use in the winter. You'll want to wear gloves since this is the time when bees are the most defensive and will protect their honey.

There really isn't much to do with bees until the end of summer. During the start of summer, the bees do most of the work. You can expect to spend about eight to ten hours with your bees in the summer, most of which will be spent harvesting and bottling honey.

IN FALL

As days become shorter and the weather cools in autumn, nectar and pollen sources become scarce. As the season slows down, so do your beehive activities.

The queen's egg-laying dramatically reduces, drones start to disappear, and the hive's population significantly drops. Bees start bringing in propolis, using it to seal up the cracks that can leak cold in the winter. The fall is the time when the hive starts preparing for winter, and you need to help them get ready. Robbing occurs most often during this time since other bees are looking to steal honey.

✓ Inspect your hive and be sure the queen is still in there. Finding eggs mean the queen was present at least two days ago.

✓ Make sure the bees have enough honey. Ideally, the upper deep hive body should be full of honey. For a cooler, northern climate a hive will need about 60 pounds or more of honey for the winter while in locations with shorter or nonexistent winters you will need about 30 to 40 pounds of honey.

✓ Medicate and feed your colony. You can feed a 2-to-1 sugar-syrup until the colder weather draws them into a tight cluster. Once they cluster the bees won't leave so, you won't need to feed them.

- ✓ You can treat your colony with Terramycin or Tylan as a precaution against AMB and EFD disease.

- ✓ Make sure your hive has proper ventilation. During winter, the center of the cluster maintains a temperature of 90 to 93 degrees Fahrenheit. Without proper ventilation, the warm air will rise, hit the inner cover which is cold, and condensation in the form of ice-cold water will drip onto the bees.

- ✓ Consider wrapping the hive in black tar paper if you're in a place that drops below freezing for more than a few weeks. Don't cover the entrance or any upper ventilation holes. The paper will absorb heat from the sun and help the colony to regulate temperatures better during the cold periods. It will also help provide a windbreak.

- ✓ If you live in a harsh winter location, you also want to provide a windbreak. You may have already been able to locate your hive near a natural windbreak, but if not, you can build one with fence posts and burlap positioned to block prevailing winds.

✓ You'll want to place a mouse guard at the front entrance to the hive.

In the fall, you can expect to spend about three to five hours feeding, medicating, and preparing your bees for the winter ahead.

IN THE WINTER

During the winter, not much happens in the hive; the queen stays warm amid the cluster of worker bees. The winter cluster begins in the brood chamber once the ambient temperature is 54 to 57 degrees Fahrenheit. Once the cold weather comes, the cluster forms within the center of the two hive bodies.

It will cover the top bars of the frames in the lower chamber and extend over and beyond the bottom bars in the food chamber. While the temperature outside may be freezing, the center of a winter cluster of bees will constantly remain 92 degrees Fahrenheit. This is because the bees generate heat by shivering their wing muscles.

There are no drones in the hive in winter, but some worker broods will start appearing in the later months of winter. Over the winter months, the bees will consume about 50 to 60 pounds of honey. The bees eat while in the cluster, moving around whenever the temperature rises above 40 to 45 degrees Fahrenheit. The bees will move to a new honey area once the weather is warm enough to leave the cluster.

WINTER TO DO LIST

✓ Monitor the hive entrance, keeping dead bees or snow from blocking it.

✓ Make sure there is enough food for the bees; this is when bees can die of starvation. To check for food, it's best if you don't remove any frames and only look inside on a day with no wind and mild weather. You may need to start some emergency feedings if you don't notice any honey in the top frames. If you start feeding the bees, you can't stop until they are bringing their nectar and pollen back to the hive.

✓ Clean, repair, and store any equipment not used in the winter.

✓ Order package bees and equipment if needed.

✓ Spend time on your bee-related hobbies, such as making beeswax, brewing mead, etc.

You won't be doing much with your bees in the winter. You will often spend two to three hours repairing equipment, plus whatever time you spend on hobbies and making products.

IN THE SPRING

This is the busiest time of the year for beekeepers. It is when new colonies are started and established colonies begin again. As the days are milder and longer, the hive comes alive, and the population booms. The queen starts laying more eggs, culminating in their highest egg-laying rate. Drones come back to the hive, and activity starts again. The pollen and nectar come in thick and fast.

✓ You want to inspect your colony as early in the spring as possible. The exact timing will depend on your location. The basic rule of thumb is that if the weather is cold enough for you to wear a heavy coat, you shouldn't inspect your hive.

✓ Make sure your bees make it through winter. The bees should be clustered relatively high in the upper deep hive body. If you can't see them, you should at least be able to hear them.

✓ Ensure you still have a queen. Look between the frames for any brood. This tells you the queen is present. If you need a better view, you should carefully remove a frame from the center of the top deep.

✓ You also want to make sure the bees still have food. See if you find any honey between the frames. The honey will be capped with white or tan cappings for the brood. If you see honey, you're fine; if not, you need to start emergency feeding your bees.

✓ Medicate and feed your colony a few weeks before the first blossoms start. You should do this whether you still have honey.

✓ Reverse your hive bodies.

✓ Anticipate your colony's growth. Add a queen excluder and honey supers to create more room for bees before the colony becomes too crowded. At this point, remove the feeder and stop all medication.

✓ Keep your eye out for swarming. Inspect regularly and look for signs of swarm cells.

Spring is the busiest time for you as a beekeeper, so you should anticipate spending about 12 hours tending bees.

Along with these seasonal tasks, it is also crucial to inspect your hive regularly to ensure smooth operation.

BEEHIVE INSPECTIONS

The more you visit your hive, the more you'll get in the habit of conventional beekeeping. When inspecting your hive, you want to look at the following things:

✓ Observe the bees coming and going from the entrance. Are they expected, or are they fighting or stumbling around without direction?

✓ Smoke the hive under the cover and at the entrance.

✓ If you have a screened bottom board, check the slide-out tray for signs of varroa mites and determine if treatment is needed. Otherwise, clean and replace the tray.

✓ Open the hive and remove the wall frame, setting it aside.

✓ Work your way through all the remaining frames.

- ✓ Look for the queen or eggs. If you find eggs, you know you have a queen. If you are positive there are no eggs, you have no queen and will need to order a new queen from a supplier.

- ✓ Look at any uncapped larvae. They should be bright white and glistening. If they are tan and dull, then you have a problem.

- ✓ Observe the brood pattern. It should be compact, with a few empty cells covering most of the frame.
- ✓ If the brood pattern is spotty with many empty cells or if the cappings are sunken in or perforated, then you have a problem.

- ✓ Look for swarm cells and provide the colony with more room to expand as needed along with adequate ventilation.

- ✓ Consider anticipating colony growth and providing the needed honey supers or moving your follow board. You should give extra room before it's obvious they need it.

Now that you know what to look for, you must consider how to inspect correctly. There are specific procedures you'll follow while looking for the above things.

STEP-BY-STEP INSPECTION

Always start your inspection by removing the first frame or wall frame. This is the frame closest to the outer wall. It doesn't matter which wall; you simply want to pick a wall to work from and proceed in the following manner:

1. Insert the curved end of your chosen hive tool between the first and second frames near one end of the frame's top bar.

2. Twist the tool to separate the frames.

3. Repeat this motion on the other end of the top bar.

4. Using both of your hands, pick up the first frame by the end bars.

After removing the first frame, gently rest it on the

ground, leaning it vertically against the hive. You can also buy the optional frame rest accessory to temporarily store the frame while you inspect the hive.

Loosen frame two with your hive tool and move it into the open slot where the first frame was. This gives you enough room to remove the frame without causing injury to any bees. Once you've finished inspecting this frame, return it to the hive close to the wall, but do not touch it. Do not place this frame on the ground.

Work through all the frames in your hive, moving each frame into the open spot. Once you've finished looking at a frame, return it snugly against the one you previously inspected. Monitor progress.

It is crucial that you hold and inspect each frame the proper way. You want your back to the sun, with the light over your shoulder and on the frame. The sun will illuminate deep into the cells so you can view larvae and eggs better. The best way to inspect both sides of the frame is with the following four-step process:

1. Hold the frame by the taps at both ends of the top bar.

2. Turn the frame so it is vertical.

3. Turn the frame like turning a page in a book.

4. Return the frame to a horizontal position, and you'll be looking at the opposite side.

After several minutes of inspection, the bees may have lined up between the top bars. This is because they are watching you. You should give a few puffs of smoke to disperse them so you can continue with the inspection.

During these inspections, you may face some common bee diseases. Let's look at what you are most likely to encounter.

COMMON BEE DISEASES

Many people don't realize that bees can become sick and suffer from various diseases when they start beekeeping. Let's look at some of the most common bee diseases and how to prevent them.

VARROA MITES

These parasites can affect both larvae and adult bees. They feed on honeybees' blood, weakening them and shortening their lifespans.

If you notice bees displaying signs such as missing legs or wings, your hive may have varroa mites. The mites seem to prefer drones so that regular inspection will prevent them. While Apistan works to eliminate varroa mites, you shouldn't use it during honey flow or if you will be harvesting honey soon for human consumption.

Foulbrood

The condition American Foulbrood is caused by the Bacillus larvae that kill the sealed broods of honeybees. The European Foulbrood isn't as big a disaster but will still deform and kill larvae. To prevent foulbrood, you must spray disinfecting spray in both spring and fall. Most beekeepers typically use Terramycin. You should not use any disinfecting medicine during honey flow or when eating the honey from a hive. If you are too late to prevent foulbrood, you'll need to destroy the colony and potentially your hive.

Colony Collapse Disorder (CCD)

No one knows for sure what causes CCD, but researchers believe it can be caused by the presence of the fungus Nosema ceranae and/or the invertebrate iridescent virus (IIV) within the hive. There is currently no solution for this problem other than burning a hive once the colony is infected.

Wintering Your Bees

Sometimes, wrapping up your hive for the winter is good; other times, it isn't recommended. In the winter, you want to help your bees defend themselves from mice and other creatures. However, you want to avoid trapping your bees.

The last thing to consider is harvesting honey.

Harvesting Honey

Most beekeepers harvest honey at the end of a substantial nectar flow and when the beehive is full of cured and capped honey. The conditions and circumstances for harvesting honey will vary greatly depending on where you live. You can only expect a small honey harvest in your first year in late summer. New colonies need a complete season to build up a large enough population to get surplus honey.

During the summer, you should look under the cover every couple of weeks. Take note of any progress your bees are making and find out how many frames are filled with capped honey. When you notice a shallow frame with 80 percent or more sealed and capped honey, you can remove and harvest the frame. Or you can leave your frames as is until one of the following happens:

➢ All the frames were filled with capped honey.
➢ The last primary nectar flow is complete for the season.

It is important to note that honey has open cells not capped with wax and can be extracted if cured. To determine if the honey has cured, turn the frame with the cells facing the ground. Give a gentle shake. If honey comes from the cells, it isn't cured and should be left on the frame. At this point, it isn't even honey; nectar isn't cured. This is because the water content is too high to be considered honey. If you try to bottle the nectar, you will only get watery syrup that will spoil and ferment.

It is essential to be patient and wait until the bees have gathered all the honey possible. However, you must also be careful not to leave the honey supers on the hive too long. If you wait too long, two things can happen:

1. Once the last primary nectar flow is done, with winter on the horizon, the bees will start to eat the honey. If you leave the supers on too long, the bees will eat much of the honey you wanted to harvest. The bees can also start to move the honey to open cells in the lower deep hive bodies. Either way, you will be losing honey that you can harvest.

2. If you wait too long, the weather will turn cold, and it will be too late to harvest your honey. In cool weather, the honey will thicken or even granulate, making it impossible to remove from the comb. Honey is easiest to harvest when it is still warm from summer and flows easily.

Here is a popular YouTube video on how to harvest honey. Look.

https://www.youtube.com/watch?v=yAuk3-5RU9Y

CHOOSING EXTRACTION EQUIPMENT

When you are ready to harvest your honey, you must have the appropriate tools and equipment. You can get your tools from a beekeeping supplier, but you can also use a couple of homemade tools.

An extractor is essentially a device that spins honey from the comb via centrifugal force. These are available in a range of sizes and styles to meet your needs and budget. Choose a model that accommodates at least four frames at a time.

You don't necessarily need to buy an extractor. Some beekeeping clubs will rent out extractors for use during harvest season. Call around to see what options are available to you before buying one. However, if you are going to start a business from honey products, then it may be best to invest in your honey extractor.

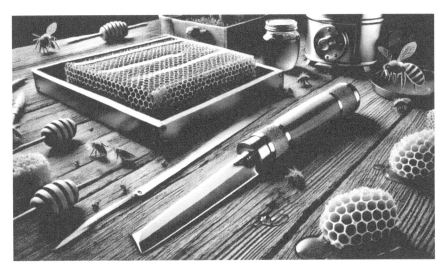

The wax cappings on honey will form an airtight seal on honey-containing cells. Before you can extract honey, you need to remove these lids. The best way to do this is with an uncapping knife.

These electrically heated knives cleanly and quickly cut through cappings. You can also choose to use a large, serrated bread knife heated by dipping it in hot water, but make sure you don't get any water into your honey.

Once you extract the honey, you must strain it before you bottle it. This process helps remove bits of wax, wood and the occasional bee. You can use any type of kitchen strainer or fine-sieved colander. You can also buy a stainless-steel honey strainer from a bee supplier designed specifically for this purpose.

DOUBLE UNCAPPING TANK

This is a helpful device that you don't really need, but it can collect the wax cappings as you remove them from the comb. This can give your business another product source.

THE PROCESS OF COLLECTING HONEY

Once you have your equipment, you must learn how to harvest your honey. It is essential to ensure you have the proper clothing and equipment before harvesting your honey. When collecting honey, you want to keep the following information in mind.

You can keep bees calm with gentle and calm movements rather than big, exaggerated moves. This will make it easier to maneuver the supers and harvest your honey. You should also avoid wearing perfumes, colognes, aftershaves, etc.; this will entice curious bees and make it harder for you to harvest honey. Harvesting honey requires the following significant steps:

1. Use smoke sparingly since it will impact the flavor of the honey. You can gently remove bees from supers with a brush.

2. Remove the honey supers.

3. Remove honey from the comb by uncapping the wax on the comb.

4. Strain the honey to remove excess wax and debris.

5. Keep the honey in a settling tank for two to three days so the air bubbles pop and foreign objects rise to the top, allowing you to remove them.

6. Skim off any foam.

7. Your process will determine the temperature at which you can keep the honey. This will help you decide what jars and containers to keep the honey in until you sell it.

EXTRACTING WAX

The capping you remove will represent most of your yearly wax harvest when you harvest your honey. You'll likely get one or two pounds of wax per 100 pounds of honey. The wax can be cleaned and melted for a variety of uses and products. Often, wax is worth more than honey, so you should work to reclaim it. Consider the following to help you extract wax from your hive.

1. Allow gravity to drain as much honey from the cappings as possible for at least a few days. A double uncapping tank can simplify the process.

2. Place the drained cappings in a five-gallon plastic pail and top off with warm water. Use a paddle to

slosh the cappings to wash off any remaining honey. Drain the cappings through a colander or a honey strainer and repeat the process until the water clears.

3. Place the capping in a double boiler and melt the wax. Always use a double boiler for this process since beeswax is highly flammable. Also, never leave melting wax unattended.

4. Strain the melted beeswax through several layers of cheesecloth to remove debris. Remelt and restrain as necessary until all impurities are removed.

5. You can pour the rendered wax into a block mold to use later.

Now that we've examined what goes into beekeeping, let's consider what you can do with your hive and the benefits you can enjoy with honey.

BENEFITS OF HONEY

You may think you already know all there is to know about honey, but to truly understand how you can turn beekeeping into a business, you want to have a basic understanding of what honey is and some basic facts.

WHAT IS HONEY?

Honey is basically condensed nectar from flower blossoms. Nectar is a sugary liquid secreted by blossoms to attract pollinating insects like honeybees.

While honeybees take nectar from a flower when they visit, the flower also gets something in return. As honeybees collect nectar, they intentionally and unintentionally collect pollen from the flower and deposit it on another flower. This ensures seed production and allows the flower species to continue growing.

NECTAR INTO HONEY

When a honey bee returns to the hive with nectar, it is processed into honey. The most significant change at this point is the considerable moisture reduction in the nectar. This causes the nectar to change from a water-like consistency into a syrup-like consistency of honey.

While there is more to the process, I'm not going to take the time to explain the entire scientific method in this book since we are more focused on the practice of beekeeping and turning it into a successful backyard business.

TYPES OF HONEY

If you're like me, you used to think all honey is the same. Then, when I started looking into beekeeping, I realized that the type of plant that sources the nectar could impact on your honey's color, flavor, aroma, and consistency. This means there is a wide range of varieties when it comes to honey. Consider an example of just two common types.

Buckwheat honey is very thick, strong-flavored and dark—almost black. On the other hand, there is alfalfa honey, which is very delicate, with a mild flavor and a water-white color. This is just an example of the difference; there are easily thousands of different types of honey.

Just as there are many types of honey, there are just as many uses.

USES OF HONEY

Honey can be used for a lot of things besides a sweet treat. Consider just a few options for honey.

- ✦ Butter
- ✦ Honey sticks
- ✦ Glaze
- ✦ Candy
- ✦ Wine
- ✦ Lip balm
- ✦ Lotion
- ✦ Moisturizing cream

✧ Soap

There are various ways that honey can be used and multiple products you can sell because of your beekeeping.

If you are going to sell honey, you must know the benefits of honey so you can market it to potential customers.

HONEY NUTRITION

Before beekeeping, I wasn't aware of honey's truly nutritional properties. Honey has some surprisingly major dietary value while giving you a sweet treat. Let's consider some of the nutritional benefits of honey.

Honey is made primarily of water and sugar. The two principal sugars are glucose and fructose. Some other ingredients in honey include galactose, maltose, and sucrose. In addition, there are several minerals and vitamins in honey.

Honey contains the following vitamins:

- B6
- C
- Riboflavin
- Niacin
- Pantothenic Acid
- Choline
- Betaine
- Pyridoxine

Honey contains the following minerals:

- Calcium
- Iron
- Phosphorus
- Potassium
- Sodium
- Zinc
- Copper
- Manganese
- Magnesium
- Sulfur
- Fluoride
- Selenium

In addition, honey is also high in the following

amino acids:

- ❖ Tryptophan
- ❖ Threonine
- ❖ Isoleucine
- ❖ Lysine
- ❖ Phenylalanine
- ❖ Tyrosine
- ❖ Valine
- ❖ Arginine
- ❖ Aspartic Acid
- ❖ Glutamic Acid
- ❖ Glycine
- ❖ Proline
- ❖ Serine

While this doesn't mean you'll get your daily recommended dose in a small teaspoon of honey, you will get more than sugar when choosing honey as an alternative to less healthy sweeteners.

CALORIES IN HONEY

A lot of people today are focused on counting calories. For this reason, it is essential to note that honey is a calorically dense food. If you eat a single teaspoon of honey, you are getting 22 calories, while table sugar only has 16 calories in a teaspoon. But this doesn't necessarily make honey bad. Honey is sweeter than sugar, so you'll probably use less.

DIFFERENT KINDS OF HONEY

It is also important to note that the nutritional benefits of honey will vary depending on the type of honey. For example, honey that is highly processed through heating or pressure filtering will have diminished nutritional properties. Highly processed honey is a clear product with a long shelf life.

While there is nothing wrong with processed honey, it isn't the same as the product that bees initially produced. Processed honey isn't nasty for you, but it isn't as beneficial as raw honey. There is also a variance in the nutritional value of honey based on the nectar source of your honey.

ADDITIONAL BENEFITS

There are also other health benefits to honey besides the vitamins and minerals. Honey is high in antioxidants and can even be used as a natural antibiotic. Let's look more closely at a few primary health benefits of honey.

29 WAYS TO USE HONEY AS MEDICINE

Honey is one of the most potent wonders of the world when it comes to healing sick minds and bodies. Here are some ways that you can use honey to treat common ailments.

HONEY IMPROVES DIGESTION AND CURES ULCERS

A simple teaspoon of pure, raw, organic honey can relieve indigestion after a meal. Consult with your doctor before using this remedy, especially if you have diabetes. If you have ulcers, it is best to use Manuka honey (from New Zealand only, where Manuka bees are from) to help treat them. You can take a tablespoon of honey as much as four times a day to treat all kinds of stomach ailments, including indigestion, gas, and nausea.

Honey & Apple Cider Drink to Fight Obesity, High Cholesterol, and High Blood Pressure

To help yourself lose weight, stir a tablespoon of honey and two tablespoons of apple cider vinegar into a glass of hot water. Drink this first thing every morning to alkalize and cleanse your digestive system and curb cravings for food throughout the week.

Drinking this weight-loss remedy every morning has been reported to help people lose two pounds a week or more. It is also effective at clearing cholesterol out of their arteries, cleansing their liver, and lowering their blood pressure.

Raw Honey & Greek Yogurt for Probiotic Support

If you have been sick with food poisoning, have been eating a lot of junk food, or have been on long courses of antibiotics, then it is very likely that your gut has been stripped of its useful bacteria.

To repopulate with the good bacteria your body needs to have a healthy immune and digestive system, mix a tablespoon with a cup of Greek yogurt and eat this mixture twice a day. It is best to use plain unsweetened yogurt for this purpose because yogurt with added sugar can only deplete good bacteria from your gut and increase the presence of harmful bacteria and yeast.

HONEY, GINGER, AND LEMON TO RELIEVE NAUSEA

Ginger is a traditional anti-nausea remedy that works well with honey to settle the stomach. This mixture is particularly good for women suffering from morning sickness. Dosing yourself with it the night before might lessen the severity of any morning sickness you might be experiencing.

This mixture is also a good one to take before a long trip if you suffer from car sickness, boat sickness, or air sickness.

Mix a tablespoon of raw grated ginger, a tablespoon of lemon juice, and a full honey. Take this mixture at the first sign of feeling nauseous as often as you need during the day. If you like, you can dilute the mixture in warm or cold soda water, making it easier to swallow. You can also bottle this mixture for long trips to handle travel sickness.

Honey & Garlic Syrup To Treat A Sore Throat

This is an ancient, effective remedy for sore throat. Chop several cloves of garlic into small chips or slices. This helps release the main antibacterial and antiviral ingredient in garlic, allicin. You can then mix this minced garlic with half a cup of honey. Let this mixture sit, capped, overnight on your counter so that the honey is infused with the garlic. For best results, take one tablespoon of the mixture every hour until your sore throat symptoms disappear.

Honey is a natural antibiotic, and Echinacea and licorice root have strong anti-inflammatory and anti-viral properties. The mixture also contains cinnamon and ginger, which are antibacterial immune fighters that help your system repair itself.

In a small saucepan, mix one cup of honey, half a cup of powdered echinacea root, two tablespoons of powdered licorice root, two tablespoons of grated ginger, half a tablespoon of cinnamon, and one cup of water. Bring the mixture to a low boil and then simmer it on low for about twenty to thirty minutes. Stir thoroughly, calm, and pour into a jar with a tight cap.

Store the mixture in the refrigerator, and take a tablespoon or two whenever you experience the first sign of a cold, flu, or cough. The mixture should last at least six months in the refrigerator, but to be on the safe side, throw it out after three months.

You can use fresh ginger, echinacea, or licorice root if you can find it. However, some people with cardiovascular issues may react to licorice root, as it can speed up the heart's rhythm. If this is true, you can completely omit it from the recipe.

Fresh ginger, echinacea and licorice roots can sometimes be obtained in natural or health food markets, Asian markets, or at old-style Caribbean apothecaries. Powdered versions of these herbs should be found at health food stores.

HONEY & LEMON DRINK FOR RESTORING THE VOICE

Add two tablespoons of honey and the juice of one large lemon to a large cup of boiling water and stir well. Drink this concoction slowly to help soothe and heal inflamed vocal cords. It can also help clear phlegm from the throat. Actors and singers created this drink to help restore their voices after a grueling evening of performing.

If you want to reduce your risk of developing plaque and gingivitis, use a honey and coconut oil plaque rinse. This type of treatment is also sometimes called a "pull" because the coconut oil pulls the bacteria out of your mouth.

Mix two ounces of coconut oil and a teaspoon of honey in a small glass. You can warm the honey slightly in the microwave for one or two seconds to make it more liquid in texture and more straightforward to pour, if necessary.

Drink the honey and coconut oil mixture and swish it in your mouth for as long as you can stand. Holding the mixture in your mouth for about eight minutes is ideal, but most people spit it out after about two minutes. Keep in mind that the longer you swish it around in your mouth and let it sit on your gums and teeth, the more plaque and bacteria will be removed.

Honey, Baking Soda & Lemon Juice for Bad Breath

Antiviral and lemons are antibacterial and antiviral substances that fight plaque and bad breath. Mix one teaspoon of raw honey with one teaspoon of lemon juice and one teaspoon of baking soda in a glass. Stir it around well, and then gargle with the mixture for at least three minutes before spitting it out.

Honey & Milk for Insomnia

Warm milk contains the amino acid L-tryptophan, a brain chemical that promotes sleep. It is the same amino acid in turkey that puts you to sleep after a big dinner. Honey is comforting and contains glucose, which also promotes relaxation and recovery.

Mix one tablespoon of honey into a glass of warm milk, and then drink it just before bedtime. This is much healthier for you than taking an addictive sleeping pill.

HONEY & BLACK TEA TO CURE A HANGOVER

One of the most effective ways to cure a hangover is to brew a strong black tea as usual and then add two tablespoons of raw honey to the mixture.

The fructose in the honey will help your body break down the toxins in your liver that result from drinking too much. You can also add a splash of milk to this if you like to help relieve the irritability that is often part of having a bad hangover.

HONEY & NETTLE TEA TO TREAT ALLERGIES

Honey contains pollen from the bees that make it from flowers. To help you deal with seasonal allergies, mix one tablespoon of local honey with a tea made with nettle leaf to reduce severe allergic reactions to pollen.

It is crucial to use locally grown honey from your area to build immunity against the pollen you are inhaling. Nettle is part of the solution to allergies because it is a natural immune booster with antihistamine qualities.

HONEY, APPLE & FLAXSEED DRINK TO LOSE WEIGHT

This nutritious, high-fiber, filling drink can help you eat less before a meal and satisfy cravings for anything sweet. The honey provides you with energy to get through your morning or afternoon, and the apple is a good source of protein. The flax and the apple are great sources of fiber, especially if you leave the peel on the apple when you blend this drink to make this weight-loss drink.

In a blender carafe, combine one chopped-up medium red apple, one tablespoon of ground flaxseeds, two tablespoons of honey, one cup of spring water or distilled water, and one cup of ice. Use this drink as a daily replacement for breakfast or lunch to cut your calories by up to 1000. This regimen can help you lose two to five pounds weekly. However, if you have a chronic health problem, be sure to consult with your doctor before going on a calorie-deprivation diet such as this one.

Honey & Cranberry Drink to Cure Urinary Tract Infections

Cranberry juice and honey have antibacterial properties that can cleanse the bladder and urinary tract of bacteria. Both foods are also anti-inflammatory, helping reduce the pain and swelling associated with bladder infections or cystitis.

Mix one tablespoon of honey with a cup of sugar-free cranberry juice and drink this every four hours until the infection clears up (at least two days). Be sure to drink at least four liters of water a day while you are on this infection-fighting regime to ensure that your body is constantly flushing the bacteria and mucus out of your bladder and urethra.

Honey & Turmeric Root Drink to Support the Liver

If you suffer from liver problems such as fatty liver, jaundice, or Hepatitis A, drinking a blend of powdered turmeric root and honey can help you recover from the ailment faster. The turmeric root powder is a potent anti-inflammatory, and the honey helps to remove fat, toxins and bile from the liver.

In a small bowl, make a thick paste of two tablespoons of turmeric powder and two tablespoons of honey. Pour boiling water into a cup and mix the paste into the water until it dissolves completely. Squeeze a wedge of lemon into the tea and add a dash of black pepper to taste.

You can make a larger batch of this and keep it in the refrigerator so you can drink it throughout the day. However, for best results when it comes to detoxifying your liver, it is recommended that you take this drink twice a day.

Honey and Apple Cider Vinegar to Combat Intestinal Parasites

If you suspect that you have intestinal parasites, consume this mixture of raw honey and apple cider vinegar twice a day. Add one tablespoon of apple cider vinegar and one tablespoon of honey to a glass of spring water and drink it.

RAW HONEY & GOAT'S MILK TO INCREASE MALE SPERM COUNT

An ancient remedy for a low sperm count still considered effective today is mixing two tablespoons of honey into a cup of raw organic goat's milk and consuming it twice a day. The proteins in the goat's milk are also powerful probiotics that keep the male reproductive system in peak health.

There has also been anecdotal evidence that taking this fertility solution twice a day also helps increase a woman's chances of conceiving a baby.

HONEY LEMON-LIME HYDRATION SPORTS DRINK

Instead of using sugar-laden commercial drinks to hydrate yourself on a hot day or after a workout, try making this healthier honey-based drink.

In a blender carafe, combine ¼ cup of fresh lime juice, ¼ cup of fresh lemon juice, 1/8 of a teaspoon of sea salt, two tablespoons of raw honey, and two cups of fresh spring water or distilled water. Whip it all with a handful of ice and drink to prepare or recover from the heat or workout.

These ingredients supply your body with the electrolytes needed to rehydrate your muscles and tissues after a workout. Take some with you in a bottle when you go for a walk on a long, hot summer's day, and never consume sports drinks with 38 grams of white sugar or more in them again.

Honey & Cinnamon Salve for Eczema

To make a homemade salve for eczema, add a teaspoon of cinnamon to half a cup of honey. Use your blender to mix the ingredients and then scoop them into a small jar if necessary.

Apply the salve to the area of skin affected by eczema. Rub the salve right into your skin if necessary. The cinnamon heats the area and draws blood to the surface of the dermis to help it eliminate toxins faster. The honey sterilizes the skin and adds moisture so that the affliction is not so itchy and flaky.

HONEY & YOGURT TO SOOTHE SUNBURN

If you have spent too much time in the sun, you can mix a quarter of a cup of honey with a quarter of a cup of yogurt and apply it to your skin. This can help cool your skin off and sterilize it so it does not get infected while it is healing. For real relief, try chilling the yogurt and honey mixture in the refrigerator before applying it to your skin.

If you do not have any yogurt on hand, you can also try applying the honey straight on the burn or mixing it with a bit of coconut oil before applying it. Coconut oil has essential fatty acids that can also help heal burned skin.

Applying a salve to any open burn with weeping blisters that ooze pus is not a good idea.

HONEY, LEMON &YOGURT FACE MASK FOR WRINKLES

This is a facemask, but you can use it anywhere

on your body that has wrinkles, such as the hands or neck. The lactic acid in the yogurt old skin cells and the honey plumps up the skin with natural moisturizers. Lemon juice contains fruit acids that help lighten skin and eliminate dark spots and acne scars.

Mix a cup of yogurt, two tablespoons of honey, and a teaspoon of lemon juice in a small bowl. Leave the mixture for about twenty minutes and then rinse it with cool water. Let your skin dry or pat it dry with a soft towel.

Honey & Oatmeal Mask for Chickenpox Scars

Honey is loaded with natural antioxidants, which help support the skin's ability to heal itself. Oatmeal is a soothing emollient that helps to smooth the skin. When combined, they can help heal chickenpox scars.

Mix one part each of raw honey, dried oatmeal and spring water. Depending on the size of the area you want to treat, this could be anywhere from one tablespoon to one cup of the mixture. Mash everything together until the oats are soft and thick, and then apply to the scarred areas of your skin.

Leave the mixture on your skin for twenty minutes before rinsing it off in the shower. Having a drain catcher at the bottom of your shower or bathtub is also suitable for catching stray oatmeal flakes so they do not clog your drain.

HONEY & BAKING SODA BATH FOR DRY, FLAKING SKIN

This bath helps moisturize and heal dry or flaky skin caused by cold weather or a very dry desert climate. Both honey and baking soda alkalinize the water, which also helps balance the skin's pH.

Add two cups of baking soda and half a cup of honey to a hot bath. Immerse yourself in it for at least twenty minutes, then pat yourself dry with a towel when you emerge from the water. Do not be tempted to use soap to rinse the mixture off your body, as that will mitigate the healing effects of the honey and baking soda.

Honey & Lavender Essential Oil Bath for Insomnia

To remedy insomnia, add two tablespoons of honey to a cup of hot water and let it dissolve. Add five drops of Lavender Essential Oil to the cup of water and swirl it around until it is well integrated with the honey.

Add the lavender and honey mixture to a bath full of hot water. Be sure to inhale the fumes of the lavender and honey while relaxing in the bath to ensure that your nasal passages also benefit from the therapeutic aromatherapy. Soak in the bathtub until your skin is hot and steamy, and when you emerge from the bath, you will be feeling very sleepy.

Honey to Heal Small Scrapes, Cuts and Bug Bites

Dab a bit of honey over a skin abrasion or bug bite to encourage a wound to heal. The sugars in the honey will promote the skin cells to knit together and heal, and the fact that honey is a natural anti-bacterial substance will help the wound heal without infection.

This is also a good thing to do if you have a small abrasion and do not have a Band-Aid to cover it. The honey will act as a disinfectant and protectant of the abrasion until you can find one.

Raw Honey for Treating Yeast Infections

Applying raw honey directly around and inside vaginal area can help get rid of yeast or vaginal infections. Apply the honey directly to the afflicted area, especially paying attention to deep skin folds, and let it sit for thirty minutes. Then, wash the honey off your body in the bath or shower and dry yourself well with a clean towel.

HONEY, NUTMEG ORANGE JUICE DRINK FOR ANXIETY

This is a recipe from the Ayurveda tradition of medicine. Mix a cup of orange juice with a tablespoon of honey and a pinch of nutmeg. Nutmeg is a natural sedative and a mild muscle relaxant. It is also a hallucinogen, so it is important not to use more than a pinch of it in each serving. Drink this mixture twice daily to help allay feelings of anxiety. You can also bottle a bit of it and take it with you into situations that might trigger social anxiety.

HONEY & CASTOR OIL TO TREAT HICCUPS

Mix a teaspoon of honey and one teaspoon of castor oil in a container with a tight lid. Shake the mixture until the honey and oil are well integrated. Dip a spoon into the mixture and lick the spoon every time you get hiccups. Both honey and castor oil relax the diaphragm and relieve the spasms associated with hiccups.

HONEY & PINEAPPLE TO CURB CRAVINGS FOR CIGARETTES

Eat a small piece of raw pineapple dipped in honey to curb cravings for cigarettes. This lovely treat will help satisfy any cravings for nicotine, which are caused by your brain's need to produce endorphins.

The treatment is sweet enough that your brain will feel like its urge has been satiated, and the craving or nicotine will disappear.

12 Ways of Using Honey for Beauty

Honey is rich in B vitamins, natural sugars, antioxidants, and polyphenols. It is an ideal cosmetic ingredient because it is nutritious, versatile, and comes in so many forms.

Honey Lip Scrub for Healing and Lip Plumping

This recipe is for raw, chapped lips; honey is a humectant that draws moisture to your lips. Mix one tablespoon of raw honey, a teaspoon of sugar, olive or coconut oil, and a dash of powdered ginger or cinnamon for flavor. Mix everything and then keep it in a small jar by your sink.

Put some on your finger and rub your lips vigorously. When dry skin is removed from your lips, rinse the mixture with cold water.

Use this mixture whenever you want to remove

dead skin or simply make your skin look plumper.

Honey & Baking Soda Cleansing Facial Scrub

This simple facial scrub removes dead skin, grease and old makeup. The honey pulls grime out of your pores, and the tiny granules of baking soda help to refine your skin. Place a teaspoon of honey on a warm, wet washcloth, then sprinkle half a cup of baking soda on top.

Scrub your face evenly and firmly with the washcloth, wetting it now and then reactivating the baking soda and honey mixture on the cloth. Once your skin feels clean, rinse it off with a splash of cold water.

Honey, Milk, Lemon & egg white Mask to Make Your Skin Glow

The ingredients in this mask stimulate your skin's circulation to make it glow. The lemon's fruit acids and the milk and egg's protein help make your skin look healthy and smooth.

In a medium-sized mixing bowl, mix a tablespoon of honey, a tablespoon of milk, two egg whites, and a tablespoon of lemon juice. Add a sprinkle of flour and keep stirring to thicken the mixture a bit so that it is easier to spread on your face.

Spread this mask on the clean, dry skin with your fingers or a Popsicle stick and leave it on for about twenty minutes before rinsing it off in the shower.

HONEY & PAPAYA ANTI-AGING MASK

The papaya in this mask contains lots of Vitamin A and fruit acids that help to resurface the skin and get rid of wrinkles. Papaya, like honey, is a substance that helps to draw moisture to the skin, making it look plumper and younger.

Use a fork and mash one small papaya with two tablespoons of honey in a bowl to make a paste. You can also mash the cubes of soft papaya together in a blender if you want. Apply the mixture to your face and leave it on for twenty minutes. Rinse the mixture off, preferably in the shower, as it could be lumpy. Do not wash your face afterward so your skin can retain the nutrients and water, attracting nutrients from the fruit and honey for hours afterward.

Note that if you are suffering from hormonal acne caused by menopause, you can add a tablespoon of yogurt or cream to the mask to help balance out and repair your skin.

HONEY & ALOE VERA MASK TO TREAT ACNE

Aloe vera is known for its skin-soothing and anti-irritant qualities, and honey helps disinfect and rebalance the skin. You can use the gel that comes directly from the aloe vera leaf or the bottled aloe vera gel that you get in the drug store or natural food store to make the mixture.

Combine two tablespoons of honey with two or more aloe vera gel and smooth it all over your face. This mixture will feel quite sticky but leave it on for about twenty minutes before rinsing it off with cool water and patting your face dry with a clean towel.

The honey in this homemade face mask disinfects and moisturizes your skin and helps remove the plugs of dirt and oil called comedones from your skin. The gelatin helps to soften and moisturize the skin, and the grapefruit contains natural sugars that help exfoliate the top layer of skin and dissolve the blackheads. The tablespoon of whipping cream in this mixture also has milk sugars that gently dissolve the top layer of skin.

In a safe microwave bowl, combine three tablespoons of unflavored gelatin powder with one tablespoon of full-fat whipping cream until smooth. Add two tablespoons of grapefruit juice and two tablespoons of honey to the mixture. Microwave the mixture for about twenty seconds, then take it out and stir it. Put it in the microwave again for another twenty minutes.

Before you apply this mixture to your skin, ensure it is not hot, or you can burn it. Be sure to use the mixture evenly anywhere that you want the blackheads removed. Apply it as thickly as possible so it will peel off your face in one piece later.

Leave the mask on your face for at least thirty minutes before peeling it off. As you lift it off, it will reveal old skin, debris, and dirt that have been clogging your pores. Once it is off, rinse your face well with cold water.

HONEY & GERANIUM ESSENTIAL OIL BATH TO SOFTEN SKIN

To soften your skin and make it glow, add two tablespoons of honey to a cup of hot water and let it dissolve. Add five drops of Geranium Essential Oil to the cup of water and swirl it around. Soak in the bathtub until your skin is hot and steamy, and when you emerge from the bath, your skin will be softer and have a special glow.

HONEY & OLIVE OIL MAKEUP REMOVER

To remove your makeup, mix a teaspoon of honey with two tablespoons in a small bowl. Dip a cotton pad or cotton ball into the mixture, not the mixture, and smooth it over your skin to help remove foundation, mascara, blush, and lipstick. The honey makes the mixture tacky enough to remove even the most stubborn makeup stains.

HONEY & OLIVE OIL NATURAL FACIAL HAIR REMOVER

Honey is a sticky substance that becomes even stickier when mixed with brown sugar. This method of hair removal has been used since ancient Egypt, and it is called "sugaring."

Mix one tablespoon of honey with three tablespoons of brown sugar in a microwave-safe bowl. Warm the mixture in the microwave for five to six seconds. The substance will be very sticky, so be sure to apply it with a Popsicle stick; otherwise, the mixture will just stick like good to your fingers.

Place a small piece of muslin cloth (or muslin bandage) over the area that needs hair removal and rub it slightly to engage any hair before pulling it back and ripping the hair out of its roots by the follicles. The facial hair will be removed, and you can see it embedded on the muslin cloth.

This hair removal method does not work well if the mixture cools, so you may have to reheat it as necessary. It also works best on lighter hair on the face. It is not as successful when removing coarse body hair or whiskers. Many women have success with removing hair from their arms with this mixture.

HONEY & SWEET ALMOND MIXTURE TO REMOVE DARK CIRCLES

Honey attracts moisture, and sweet almond oil contains fatty lipids that nourish and plump up delicate under-eye tissue.

Mix one teaspoon of honey with one teaspoon of sweet almond oil and spread the mixture beneath the eyes. Leave it on for about twenty minutes and then remove with a tissue, lightly dabbing the delicate under-eye tissue. Leave the mixture under your eyes and do not attempt to remove it by rinsing it off of your face with soap or water.

HONEY & APPLE CIDER VINEGAR TO SHINE AND STRENGTHEN NAILS

Apple cider vinegar is a nutrient-rich substance that, along with the honey, delivers B vitamins to the nail bed to help strengthen nails and protect them from infection

Mix one tablespoon of honey with one-quarter cup of vinegar in a shallow dish. Soak your nails in the mixture for ten minutes and then rinse. Repeat this soaking ritual weekly to grow and keep strong, healthy cuticles and nails.

HONEY & COCOA BUTTER CUTICLE MOISTURIZER

Mix a teaspoon of cocoa butter with a teaspoon of honey and rub the mixture over your cuticles to keep them healthy and intact. The essential fatty acids in the cocoa butter, along with the honey, help to protect and moisturize the cuticles. The honey also acts as a sealant and antibiotic, stopping cuticles from stripping and becoming infected.

HONEY PRODUCTS FOR USE AROUND THE HOME

BEESWAX AS A PROTECTIVE TREATMENT FOR LEATHER AND WOOD

When mixed with mineral oil, beeswax can be rubbed on leather or wood as a protectant. Melted beeswax with two tablespoons of carnauba and two cups of mineral spirits in a double boiler.

Stir constantly and do not let it come to a boil, as the intention here is to meld all the melted ingredients together. The mixture will cool and become lukewarm but still moldable. Molding it into a lump or ball will help make it easier to handle. You can also pour the mixture into an ice cube tray or small mold to help it take shape.

When beeswax bars or balls are solid, you can rub them on anything made of leather, such as furniture, coats, or boots, as a protectant. You can also polish a wood table with this mixture by rubbing it directly on the book and smoothing the mixture out with a cloth. This formula also works well for cutting boards.

Beeswax To Smooth Metal Rails

If the metal rails that enable drawers, screen doors or closet doors to open are sticking, rub a chunk of beeswax along the rails to make them more slippery.

Beeswax to Protect Copper and Bronze From Oxidation

Rubbing washed beeswax directly on the object to prevent copper and bronze from oxidizing. This will help prevent it from getting that moldy green look and help it retain its patina longer.

Beeswax For Smoothing Ropes

If you have rough or frayed ropes in your laundry, on your sailboat, or anywhere else, you can rub them down with a piece of raw, washed beeswax.

This makes handling rough, twisted, or thick ropes easier. Smoothing the rope with beeswax also helps it slip more easily through metal hooks or perforations and reduces its risk of "catching."

TIPS AND TRICKS FOR USING BEESWAX, HONEYCOMB & HONEY FOR HEALTH

- If you are allergic to bees, you may be allergic to beeswax, so be aware of this before you use this substance or honeycomb in honey internally or externally
- Note that it is essential not to feed honey to infants under one year of age, as they are vulnerable to a spore in honey that can cause botulism
- All honey products are naturally antibacterial and can be stored practically forever at room temperature.
- The tastiest honeycombs and honey are those that are darker in color, as they tend to have a richer flavor
- If you are using honey but not the honeycomb, do not throw it away; instead leave it in your

garden to encourage bees to build a hive around it

- Honey kept in warmer temperatures tends to darken and thicken over time, whereas honey kept in lower temperatures becomes stiffer in texture

We've got many basics, so let's get to what you came here for. Consider what it takes to start a backyard beekeeping business and how many ways you can make money from beekeeping.

Starting BEEKEEPING Business

About 450 million pounds of honey are estimated to be consumed in the United States alone each year. Yet American beekeepers only produce 149 million pounds a year. To meet demand, honey often comes from overseas locations such as Argentina, China, Germany, Mexico, Brazil, Hungary, India, and Canada.

The average consumer isn't aware that honey is one of the top foods susceptible to adulteration and fraud. To fill the gap in demand, many commercial honey producers and importers reduce the quality of honey by adding extraneous, improper, and inferior ingredients.

Some add high fructose corn syrup in order to extend honey. Others remove natural pollen through eating and ultra-filtering. This is what makes honey clear and less prone to crystallization. Filtering also makes it more difficult to trace the origin of the honey since the pollen allows the honey to be tracked to a specific floral source and the region where it was grown.

Since starting this mini backyard business, I have learned that there is a huge demand for locally produced organic and homegrown honey. Since we started, we have grown from one mini colony to over 35 colonies, and we still run out of honey every year. We are now planning to open a 3-acre, all-organic honey farm.

REGULAR VS. RAW HONEY

The main difference between regular and raw honey is that commercially produced honey is often ultra-filtered and pasteurized. Pasteurization is a process during which honey is heated at high temperatures to kill any yeast that may lead to botulism. It also prevents honey from crystallizing, making it more attractive.

However, all this heating and filtering will also destroy most of the enzymes and some vitamins while removing the beneficial pollen. It will also evaporate most of the natural aromas and flavors. This is why commercial honey doesn't have most of the health benefits or sensory delights of raw honey. Raw may not look attractive, but it will have more flavor, aroma and health benefits.

ORGANIC HONEY

You'll also find some honey labeled as organic. In the United States, the producer needs to be certified organic to put a label with this claim on it. From a business standpoint, this can be a great marketing idea, but in some cases, this claim may not be accurate.

One part of the issue is that the United States Department of Agriculture (USDA) hasn't developed a definitive guideline for organic honey yet. However, they are working to amend the current regulations that regulate the production of organic beekeeping products such as honey.

This will help establish USDA standards for managing honeybee colonies and products. The new provisions are expected to include provisions for the transition to organic apiculture production, replacement of bees, hive construction, forage areas, supplemental feeding, healthcare practices, pest-control practices and an organic apiculture system plan.

Another issue is that bees can forage nectar and pollen from flowers up to miles away from the hive, and there is no way to guarantee whether these flowering plants are subjected to chemical treatments or not. The same can be said for genetically modified plants.

Meanwhile, many people prefer backyard beekeepers and their honey products over commercial honey products. You know how the product is produced, how you care for your bees, and where the nectar comes from.

Let's consider the steps needed to start a beekeeping business and the costs involved.

STEPS TO STARTING A BEEKEEPING BUSINESS

Healthy bees can prosper year-round, so you must constantly monitor your bees and hive when you start a beekeeping business. After honey production is finished for the year, bees can still live on pollen and store honey until the following spring. Since this period can be as long as six months in cold climates, you need to make sure your bees have proper nutrition and a weather-protected hive. To start a thriving beekeeping business, you must take the following steps.

First, you want to obtain approval for zoning and homeowner's association. Go to your local zoning office to ensure there are no beekeeping restrictions within your municipal limits and obtain any written permits you need. Sure, you live within a homeowners' association. You'll also need to make sure that beekeeping is allowed within your development and document any approval.

Second, you need to develop a structure for your beekeeping business. You should consider getting the help of a Certified Public Accountant who has experience with agricultural companies. You'll also want to talk with a commercial insurance agent with a good background in liability. Contact your city or county clerk's office about getting a business license and any other permits you need. Your State Department of Revenue will be able to help you get a sales tax license for the sale of your bee-related products. An agriculture attorney will help with any state-keeping laws.

The third step is to get region-specific knowledge from a beekeeper association. This will give you invaluable support in maintaining your bee colony. They will also be able to provide you with helpful information on local bee diseases, other pests that can affect your hive, and general support information. You can even learn about the location of existing beehives and the types of honey produced in your area.

After your research, it is time to order your beekeeping equipment. As discussed earlier, you want to ensure that you have the proper protective equipment and tools needed to maintain the hive and harvest your honey.

Once all your supplies are in place, you can get the bees needed for your initial colony. Your local beekeeper's association will be able to tell you if a local member has a colony or where you can go for a starter package of bees. You can also choose to purchase your bees online.

The last step is to investigate markets for your honey and other products. As we've discussed, there are several markets and places to sell your honey. Establish a plan and determine the best places to sell your supplies.

Once you've done all this, you must keep up a good cycle. After each harvest, evaluate your entire beekeeping operation. Check the health of your bees and the entire hive, refine your maintenance techniques and compare your expenses to your revenue. Expand your supply of bees as needed to further your market growth.

COST OF STARTING BEEKEEPING

The cost of starting a beekeeping business isn't that high, and there are many ways to make money from beekeeping. Start small, in your backyard with 3-4 colonies, and see how it goes. First, bottle and sell your honey to local fruit stands and vendors. If you see good demand for it, you can consider making it a real business. You can get started for under $1,000, generating around $3,000 yearly income for you.

Here is the cost of starting a 1,000-colony operation before you get into beekeeping. Remind you that a business with 1.000 colonies is a big business and can generate hundreds of thousands of dollars.

HIVE BUILDING EQUIPMENT

1,000 bottom boards = $6,500
1,000 covers = $6,000

2,000 deep boxes = $18,000

20,000 deep frames = $9,000

20,000 deep foundations = $1,200

1,000 medium-sized boxes = $5,000

10,000 medium depth frames = $3,000

10,000 medium depth foundations = $3,500

100,000 frame eyelets = $200

2,000 queen excluders = $11,000

6,000 metal rabbets = $480

50 fume boards = $450

1 bee blower = $250

75 gallons paint = $1,500

1 staple gun and compressor = $500

1,000 packages of bees = $19,000

HONEY HANDLING EQUIPMENT

Automatic un-capper = $1,700 to $3,000

Frame conveyor = $600

Conveyor drip pan = $250

Cappings melter = $1,000 to $2,000

Extractor = $1,900 to $7,800

Settling tanks = $170 to $250 each

Spin float in place of a melter = $3,300

Honey sump = $325 to $800

Honey pump = $170 to $190

Flash heater = $1,000

Barrels = $8 to $16 each

Barrel truck = $160 to $250

Hand truck = $125 to $525

Glass jars = $17,300

Bottling equipment = $940

Of course, this is merely the cost of your supplies and equipment. Don't forget the overhead cost, renting land or working space, permits to get started, and marketing expenses.

6 Must Do's when Starting a New Business

As I've said, starting a honey-making business is easy and doesn't require much. However, I've learned from experience and talking to others in the industry that there are six specific things you need to do to get your business off to a good start.

Name Your Business

You need to get customers to distinguish your product from others in the same industry. This means you will need a business name and not just a name. You want a short name that is easy to remember while also being catchy.

You must ensure that the name you choose isn't being used by any other company. For information about business names, contact the Patent and Trademark Office.

One good way to search is by searching the name you picked on Google to see if anyone else uses it for the same purpose. My advice is if you find a good name, go ahead and buy the domain name of the name you just picked. This way, in the future, if you ever want to grow, you can have a website under that name.

You can go to Godaddy.com, name.com, or any other domain name seller's site and type the name you picked; they will tell you if that name is available for purchase with .com or .net. Typically, most domain names cost around $10/year, which, in my opinion, is a great investment.

LICENSE YOUR BUSINESS

All businesses need proper licenses to operate. This shows that you are running a legal business. However, before you are allowed to license a business, you need to determine a structure for your business. If you know an accountant or an attorney, ask them to file a legal business entity (Like an LLC,

S Corp, or LLP) on your behalf. This way, you are legally protected from most business liabilities.

You can also go on websites like leaglzoom.com and have them draw up the document for less than what an attorney would charge you to do the same.

Once you file the article to incorporate your business, the next step is to get an accountant or CPA to file and obtain an EIN(Employer's Identification Number) from the IRS. This is similar to a social security number but for businesses. Once you have these two documents, you can open a commercial bank account at any local bank.

The next step is to go to your local city office and find out what type of business and regulatory licenses you are required to have. Getting your licenses and permits should take a day or two, and then you are officially in business.

Once you have a business license and a trademark name, customers will trust your products and be more likely to buy them.

COMPETITIVE ANALYSIS OF YOUR BUSINESS

This is key to a successful business. A competitive analysis will help you determine your business's current position within the local honey-producing industry.

Competitive analysis allows you to obtain the information you need on your competitors, market share, market strategies, growth and other important factors. With this information, you will be able to change or improve your business in key areas to increase profits and sales.

Here is a simple way you can do a competitive analysis. On a piece of paper, write down the following:

1. Number of local competitors you have
2. What is their niche/what type of honey do they sell
3. Where they sell
4. What is their pricing strategy (price/oz.)

Once you have that list, take a look and see where you fit in, how you can stand out from the crowd, and what you can do differently to make customers pay attention to your products.

In my business experience, I believe there are three ways to always stand above the crowd. I have always tried to use these three strategies.

1. By making superior products than my competitors make
2. By offering a 100% customer satisfaction guarantee
3. By creative pricing strategy

Let me explain what I mean by creative pricing strategy.

CREATIVE PRICING STRATEGY

Pricing is the most crucial factor in your business. A carefully thought-out pricing strategy can make you very successful, but a pricing strategy that places you above your market can literally put you out of business. On the other hand, pricing below the market can wipe your bottom line profit completely clean, and before you know it, you are out of business and in debt.

That was the risky part; now, the tricky part is that if you stay with the market, you stand out in the crowd. Instead, you are standing in the crowd. To make yourself more visible and unique and to stand tall among competitors, you have to be very creative when it comes to your pricing strategy, and that is where the tricky part comes in. My goal is to teach you how to implement a carefully thought-out pricing strategy that can make you stand out and be successful.

Here are a few ideas I often try:

1. Always run one special where you offer a discount on one size honey bottle each month, but never the same type or size bottle every month

2. Run a BOGO (Buy One, Get One Free)
   promotion every few months on select-size
   bottles (usually those not selling fast).

3. Never try to be the low-price leader. (It is a
   slippery slope; don't try to reduce your price to
   stay competitive.)

4. Run various package promotions during
   holidays (I usually make baskets with a box of
   crackers, three bottles of our honey (all
   different sizes), one bottle of pure maple
   syrup, and one bottle of honey BBQ sauce that
   is made locally by a company who uses our
   honey, all nicely wrapped)

Remember, when it comes to pricing or marketing
ideas, there is no "one size fits all. " Not every idea
works for everyone. Some strategies may work
better for you than others and vice versa. So, it is a
good idea to test each idea separately, document the
results, and analyze them to see which worked best.

Understanding Penny Profit, Profit Margin, and Markup

These are the three most common business terms we hear every day, but what do they all mean, and how are they different from each other? Many of you have this question. I know this because I get emails about this topic from time to time.

Okay, let's break them down and see what they are:

Penny Profit

Penny profit is essentially the actual cash profit you make by selling any items in your store. For example, say you just sold a bottle of 20 oz. Coke costs $1.75; what is the penny profit from that sale? To find the answer, we need to see how much you paid to buy that bottle of Coke. Your Coke invoice shows you paid $1.00 for that bottle of Coke, and you sold it for $1.75. So, your penny profit is $1.75-1.00 = 75 cents. Penny profit is the difference between the selling price and actual costs.

PROFIT MARGIN

Profit margin is the term most widely used and understood in almost every business. It is what we all use to determine whether we are making enough profit from our businesses by selling products and services.

Profit margin is the percentage of profit you make or earn when you sell a product. Confusing? Let's look at the same example of that coke bottle we just used earlier.

We already know the penny profit from that sale was 75 cents. Now, the profit margin is done a little differently. To find out the exact margin, we will have to take the penny profit and divide that number by the selling price. So, it will be $1.75-$1.00=0.75. Then we divide that penny profit by the selling price: 0.75/$1.75 = 43% profit margin.

MARKUP

Conversely, the markup is somewhat similar to the profit margin, but instead of dividing the penny profit by the selling price, you would have to divide the penny profit by the actual cost. Let's take a look at the same example once again.

Remember our penny profit from that bottle of Coke? It was 75 cents; now we just need to divide that by the actual cost, which was $1.00, right? Let's do this: 0.75/$1.00 = 75% Markup for that same bottle of Coke.

BUSINESS FORECASTING

This is another valuable business tool if you want to have a profitable business. Business forecasting is essential to determining sales targets. A month-by-month sales forecast helps you identify problems and opportunities. An accurate sales forecast, along with a well-structured sales plan, will help you have an effective business.

These are six essential things you need to have a successful business.

LEGAL STEPS TO GET STARTED

OBTAINING YOUR EIN NUMBER FROM THE IRS

An EIN, or Employer Identification Number, is a social security or tax identification number for your business. The IRS and many other governmental agencies can identify your business via this unique nine-digit number.

Remember, you will not need this number if you choose to be the sole proprietor of your business.

It is simple to apply. You can do it yourself or get your accountant to do it. The process is simple: You fill out the SS-4 form, which can be filed online, via Fax, or via mail.

Here is a link to the IRS website to download or fill out the form online.

https://www.irs.gov/businesses/small-businesses-self-employed/how-to-apply-for-an-ein

---

Form **SS-4**	**Application for Employer Identification Number**	OMB No. 1545-0003
(Rev. January 2010) Department of the Treasury Internal Revenue Service	(For use by employers, corporations, partnerships, trusts, estates, churches, government agencies, Indian tribal entities, certain individuals, and others.) ► See separate instructions for each line. ► Keep a copy for your records.	EIN

Type or print clearly.

1. Legal name of entity (or individual) for whom the EIN is being requested

2. Trade name of business (if different from name on line 1)　　3. Executor, administrator, trustee, "care of" name

4a. Mailing address (room, apt., suite no. and street, or P.O. box)　　5a. Street address (if different) (Do not enter a P.O. box.)

4b. City, state, and ZIP code (if foreign, see instructions)　　5b. City, state, and ZIP code (if foreign, see instructions)

6. County and state where principal business is located

7a. Name of responsible party　　7b. SSN, ITIN, or EIN

8a. Is this application for a limited liability company (LLC) (or a foreign equivalent)?　☐ Yes　☐ No　　8b. If 8a is "Yes," enter the number of LLC members ►

8c. If 8a is "Yes," was the LLC organized in the United States?　☐ Yes　☐ No

9a. Type of entity (check only one box). Caution. If 8a is "Yes," see the instructions for the correct box to check.
- ☐ Sole proprietor (SSN) _____
- ☐ Partnership
- ☐ Corporation (enter form number to be filed) ►
- ☐ Personal service corporation
- ☐ Church or church-controlled organization
- ☐ Other nonprofit organization (specify) ►
- ☐ Other (specify) ►
- ☐ Estate (SSN of decedent)
- ☐ Plan administrator (TIN)
- ☐ Trust (TIN of grantor)
- ☐ National Guard　☐ State/local government
- ☐ Farmers' cooperative　☐ Federal government/military
- ☐ REMIC　☐ Indian tribal governments/enterprises
- Group Exemption Number (GEN) if any ►

9b. If a corporation, name the state or foreign country (if applicable) where incorporated　| State　| Foreign country

10. Reason for applying (check only one box)
- ☐ Started new business (specify type) ►
- ☐ Hired employees (Check the box and see line 13.)
- ☐ Compliance with IRS withholding regulations
- ☐ Other (specify) ►
- ☐ Banking purpose (specify purpose) ►
- ☐ Changed type of organization (specify new type) ►
- ☐ Purchased going business
- ☐ Created a trust (specify type) ►
- ☐ Created a pension plan (specify type) ►

11. Date business started or acquired (month, day, year). See instructions.

12. Closing month of accounting year

13. Highest number of employees expected in the next 12 months (enter -0- if none). If no employees expected, skip line 14.

14. If you expect your employment tax liability to be $1,000 or less in a full calendar year and want to file the Form 944 annually instead of Forms 941 quarterly, check here. (Your employment tax liability generally will be $1,000 or less if you expect to pay $4,000 or less in total wages.) If you do not check this box, you must file Form 941 for every quarter. ☐

Agricultural	Household	Other

15. First date wages or annuities were paid (month, day, year). Note. If applicant is a withholding agent, enter date income will first be paid to nonresident alien (month, day, year) ►

16. Check one box that best describes the principal activity of your business.
- ☐ Construction　☐ Rental & leasing　☐ Transportation & warehousing　☐ Accommodation & food service
- ☐ Real estate　☐ Manufacturing　☐ Finance & insurance
- ☐ Health care & social assistance　☐ Wholesale-agent/broker
- ☐ Wholesale-other　☐ Retail
- ☐ Other (specify) ►

17. Indicate principal line of merchandise sold, specific construction work done, products produced, or services provided.

18. Has the applicant entity shown on line 1 ever applied for and received an EIN?　☐ Yes　☐ No
If "Yes," write previous EIN here ►

Third Party Designee	Complete this section only if you want to authorize the named individual to receive the entity's EIN and answer questions about the completion of this form.	
	Designee's name	Designee's telephone number (include area code)
	Address and ZIP code	Designee's fax number (include area code)

Under penalties of perjury, I declare that I have examined this application, and to the best of my knowledge and belief, it is true, correct, and complete.　Applicant's telephone number (include area code)

Name and title (type or print clearly) ►

Applicant's fax number (include area code)

OPENING A COMMERCIAL BANK ACCOUNT

This is one crucial step, but it can only be done after you have a fully executed article of incorporation approved by the state and an EIN assigned by the IRS.

Once you have these two documents, you should be able to open your first commercial bank account at a bank.

But remember to check and understand various types of commercial checking account fees. You want to find a bank that offers a free or almost free commercial checking account because some larger banks can charge you hundreds of dollars each month, depending on how many transactions you make.

Ask and shop around before you sign on the dotted line.

Incorporating Your Business

When you choose a legal entity for your honey-producing business, there are two main factors to consider:

1. What your long-term goal is
2. The type of business model you intend to build

Often, you can file as a limited liability company (LLC), general partnership, or even sole proprietorship. A sole proprietorship is the ideal business structure for someone starting a food-related business, especially if it is a moderate start from home. However, most prefer the benefits of an LLC.

If you plan to expand your honey business to other locations or potentially start selling online, you don't want to file as a sole proprietor. In this instance, you should file as an LLC.

When you file as an LLC, you can protect yourself from personal liability. This means that if anything goes wrong while operating your business, only the money you invested in the company is at risk. This isn't the case if you file as a sole proprietor or a general partnership. LLCs are simple and flexible to operate since you won't need a board of directors, shareholder meetings, or other managerial formalities to run your business.

Here are all the legal business structures you can choose from. Getting advice from your CPA, accountant, or attorney is best.

BUSINESS STRUCTURE

When starting a business, there are five different business structures you can choose from:

✧ Sole Proprietor
✧ Partnership
✧ Corporations (Inc. or Ltd.)
✧ S Corporation
✧ Limited Liability Company (LLC)

SOLE PROPRIETOR

This is not the safest structure for an auto dealership business. It is used for a company owned by a single person or a married couple. Under this structure, the owner is personally liable for all business debts and may file on their income tax.

PARTNERSHIP

This is another inexpensive business structure to form. It often requires an agreement between two or more individuals who will jointly own and operate a business.

The agreement requires the partners to share all aspects of the business. Partnerships don't pay taxes but must file an informational return. Individual partners then report their share of profits and losses on their tax returns.

CORPORATIONS (INC. OR LTD.)

This is one of the more complex business structures and has the highest startup costs. Since stocks are involved, it isn't very common among small food-related businesses.

Profits are taxed at the corporate level and again when distributed to shareholders. When you build a business at this level, lawyers are often involved.

S CORPORATION

This is one of the most popular types of business entity people form to avoid double taxation. It is taxed similarly to a partnership entity. However, an S Corp. needs to be approved to be classified as such, so it isn't very common among small or home-based businesses.

LIMITED LIABILITY COMPANY (LLC)

This is the most common business structure among most startup businesses. It benefits small businesses since it reduces the risk of losing all your assets in case of a lawsuit. It provides a clear separation between business and personal assets.

You can also elect to be taxed as a corporation, which saves you money come tax time.

If you are unsure which specific business structure you should choose, you can discuss it with an accountant. They will direct you to the best possible option for your business goals.

Here is a sample article of incorporation for an LLC entity. Remember, this is just a sample. If you do decide to get incorporated, you should hire an attorney or ask your accountant to help you navigate this. Another thing to remember is that the requirements may vary widely based on your state laws.

Sample Articles of Incorporation

STATE OF ALABAMA:

COUNTY OF BALDWIN:

ARTICLES OF ORGANIZATION
OF
B&B Honey Farm LLC

The undersigned, acting as organizers of the B&B Auto Brokers LLC under the Alabama Limited Liability Company Act, adopt the following Articles of Organization for said Limited Liability Company.

Article I
Name of the Company

The limited liability company's name is B&B Honey Farm LLC (the "Company").

Article II
Period of Duration

The duration period is ninety (90) years from the filing date of these Articles of Organization with the

Alabama Secretary of State unless the Company is sooner dissolved.

Article III
Purpose of the Company

The Company is organized to engage in all legal and lawful purposes of a food-producing business.

Article IV
Registered Office and Agent

The Company's registered office is at 123 Main Court, Daphne, Alabama 36561; and the name and the address of the Company's initial registered agent is John Doe, 123 Main Court, Daphne, Alabama 36561

Article V
Members of the Organization

There is one (1) member, all of whom are identified in Exhibit A attached hereto and a part hereof. The initial capital contribution agreed to be made by both members is also listed in Exhibit A. The members have not agreed to make any additional contributions but may agree to do so in the future upon the terms and conditions outlined in the Operating Agreement.

Article VI
Additional Members

The members, as identified in the Company's Operating Agreement, reserve the right to admit additional members and determine the Capital Contributions of such Members. Notwithstanding the foregoing, the extra Members may not become managing unless and until selected to such position as provided in Article VII of the Company's Operating Agreement.

Article VII
Contribution Upon Withdrawal of Members

The members shall have the right to continue the company upon the death, retirement, resignation, expulsion, bankruptcy or dissolution of a member or occurrence of any event which terminates the continued membership of a member in the Company (collectively, "Withdrawal"), as long as there is at least One remaining member, and the remaining member agree to continue the Company by unanimous written consent within 90 days after the Withdrawal of a Member, as outlined in the Operating Agreement of the Company.

Article VIII
Manager

The name and business address of the initial manager is:

John Doe

B&B Honey Farm LLC
123 Main Court
Daphne, Alabama 36561
The Members may remove and replace the manager as provided in the Operating Agreement.

IN WITNESS WHEREOF, the undersigned have caused these Articles of Organization to be executed this ……………. Day of ………………………. 2010

_____

_____

B&B Honey Farm LLC
DATE

AN ALABAMA CORPORATION

BY: John Doe

ITS: Managing Member

This instrument was prepared by:

Jane Doe

999 Super Ct

Daphne, Al 36561

EXHIBIT A

MEMBERS INTEREST	INTIAL CONTRIBUTION
John Doe Rendered	Future Services 100%

BEESWAX

Another product often overlooked by honey is beeswax. Beeswax has several potential applications in starting a beekeeping business.

WHAT IS BEESWAX?

Beeswax is a rather complex material, and it wasn't until the 1960s that scientists were able to analyze it accurately and answer all the questions related to its composition.

The composition of beeswax was found to consist of hundreds of chemical compounds, including hydrocarbons, esters, triesters, acid polyesters, fatty acids and even some alcohol. These ingredients aren't all that interesting; rather, what they can combine to do.

PROPERTIES OF BEESWAX

Beeswax has some unique properties that have made it invaluable for various uses throughout history.

STABILITY

The chemicals that make up beeswax make it very stable and virtually unaffected by the passage of time. Archaeologists have even found ancient tombs with beeswax that is still pliable and usable after thousands of years.

INSOLUBLE IN WATER

Beeswax isn't affected by water, which makes it excellent for several waterproofing properties. Shipwrecks have been found with beeswax in perfect condition even after being submerged in water for years. When used as a polish, beeswax can help seal out water. During World War II, beeswax was frequently used to waterproof equipment such as tents, ignition systems, and ammunition.

HIGH MELTING POINT

Beeswax has one of the highest melting points of all natural waxes at 145 to 150 degrees Fahrenheit.

Beeswax is also a popular source for making candles. At one time, it was the only available source. Today, beeswax candles are highly prized since they burn cleanly with a bright, white and compact flame. They also don't smoke or produce an unpleasant odor.

The honeycomb results from a combination of beeswax's properties and the bees' skills. Beeswax comes from the blood worker bees release from glands on the abdomen.

Today, beeswax is still a highly valued commodity. While the most obvious is for making candles, plenty of other uses exist. Consider some of the applications for beeswax:

- ✓ Cosmetics: facial creams, lipsticks, lotions, and soaps.
- ✓ Pharmaceuticals: lip balm, salves, ointments and pill coatings.
- ✓ Floor and furniture polish.
- ✓ Crayons.

- ✓ Grinding and polishing optical lenses.
- ✓ Candy and chewing gum production.
- ✓ Crafting dentures, crowns, bridges and other dental equipment.
- ✓ The manufacture of lubricants.
- ✓ Grafting wax in horticulture.
- ✓ Manufacture of adhesives.

BEE POLLEN

In addition to honey, bee pollen can be another source of income for the backyard beekeeper. Many people use bee pollen supplements for the health benefits they offer. There are also several other uses for bee pollen. Let's look at the various uses for bee pollen to see how you can add this product to your business venture.

BENEFITS OF BEE POLLEN

Honeybees are responsible for nearly one-third of food production. This is because bees pollinate many of the plants that produce foods, gathering pollen and nectar from various plants.

Honeybees eat pollen and honey throughout their lives. Pollen provides bees with their only source of protein, and honey gives them all the vitamins and minerals they need to survive. This is why honeybees work hard to gather pollen and, as a by-product, produce food for the rest of us.

HOW BEE POLLEN IS COLLECTED

A honey bee colony relies on gathering pollen. For a worker bee, nothing is more serious than finding pollen sources and collecting a load to bring back to the hive. The worker bee's body is covered with many tiny hairs, each with short side-branches like a feather. The hairs collect the pollen grains as the bee works inside a flower blossom. Eventually, the bee's entire body becomes covered with pollen grains.

As the hairs become loaded with pollen grains, the bees use brush-like hairs on their legs to move the pollen grains to their hind legs. As the pollen is gathered from the body, it is dampened slightly by honey or nectar in the mouth. The pollen is packed into baskets on their hind legs, made from long, curved hairs.

Once the bees have a good-sized pollen ball on each hind leg, they can return to the hive and deposit their pellets in a honeycomb cell.

HARVESTING BEE POLLEN

Since many people believe, there are benefits to bee pollen, there is an available market for backyard beekeepers to harvest and sell bee pollen. You can harvest pollen from your hives using pollen traps. These traps are designed to remove the pollen pellets from the bees' hind legs as they pass through the narrow hive opening.

The pellets then fall into a screened container so the bees can't retrieve the pollen. The pollen can then be harvested daily. You must ensure you don't harvest too much pollen since it can harm the colony. If you have a substantial colony, it can gather more pollen than it needs so that you can harvest some.

Another option you can consider is customizing your honey to make it stand out from the rest on the market.

Making Custom Honey

Unless you can plant specific flower species on a farm with acres of land, your honeybees will collect nectar from different species of flowers, resulting in honey with a blend of nectar from various flowers. This type of honey is known as wildflower honey and is the most common type produced by backyard beekeepers.

Sometimes, a beekeeper harvests honey that only comes from one floral source, which results in something known as varietals or uni-floral honey. However, this requires acres of a single flower source and relies on the bees preparing to work the bloom when it starts producing nectar.

However, if you can take this focused approach, you will have honey with a distinctive flavor profile from a specific flower or region. No matter what you choose to sell, it is essential to brand and market your product appropriately.

How to Brand and Sell Honey

Once you start backyard beekeeping, you'll soon want to sell your honey. You'll first want to consider the branding you'll put on your honey. Honey of sale can be a nice supplement to your full-time income, and with a moderately sized beekeeping operation, you're likely to have more money than you can eat anyway.

Finding an Attractive Label

The best way to enhance the appearance and salability of your honey is to have an attractive label. The label is also the location for valuable information about the type of honey you are selling and who packaged it. You can often find generic labels from a beekeeping supplier, but you may want to choose to make your custom label.

One of the cheapest places we found where we had our initial label design is an online site called

Fiverr.com. This a site where you can find many designers and other talents for only $5. Our first label was designed for $5 only. We then took that design to a local printer and had them print 1000 labels.

When making your honey label, there are three things you are required to put on your label:

1. You must state what the container contains, in this case, honey.
2. You must include your name and address as the producer.
3. You must report the net weight on the lower 20 percent of the label with a dual weight system. For example, the NET WEIGHT is 16 OZ. (1 lb.). This is mandated by federal law.

In addition to these three requirements, some things you should include on the label are the following:

➢ Information on the type of honey in the package and a statement on honey's purity and wholesome nature.

➤ Information about nutritional value.

WHERE TO MARKET YOUR HONEY

You will have an independently owned food market in your area that may be interested in selling your local honey. Since honey is a pure and natural food, there is no requirement for a license to package and sell it. Some other places to consider selling your honey include the following:

❖ Health food stores often want a source of fresh, local honey.
❖ Gift stores, craft shops, and boutiques often sell honey or other bee-related products.
❖ You can sell directly from your front yard.
❖ Local farmers' markets will allow you to set up a stand.
❖ Church fairs, synagogue bazaars, and gardening centers are other locations where you can set up a booth.
❖ And don't forget word of mouth; offer bottles to your neighbors, and soon word will start spreading.

MARKETING YOUR HONEY

Marketing honey can be a bit of a challenge since there are a lot of commercial honey sellers with a lot of resources to promote and market their products. Part of your marketing strategy should be to open an online store since this is the easiest option for many backyard beekeepers. However, this also means that you will need an effective system for packing and shipping your honey to the rest of the world.

When selling honey online, you need to be capable of handling online orders yourself, or you need to be prepared to subcontract to a company that can pack and ship your honey, so you don't have to deal with it yourself.

When it comes to marketing, it helps you to learn the little things so your business will be more successful. Soon, you'll know what you need to turn your backyard beekeeping into a thriving business. Business promotion isn't a skill that is easy to learn, and you'll need to focus on it in order to persist and make your business a success.

Thankfully, you are working with honey, a product that is in demand and people want to buy. Having a detailed marketing plan will help you adjust as your beekeeping grows and you discover new markets to sell your beekeeping products.

It is a good idea to have a website. This allows you to grow your business and reach a deeper customer market than simply selling to locals from a stand. This is why many smaller businesses turn into larger companies, but you'll need the right tools to improve your business exposure.

So, there you have it. Starting a beekeeping business in your backyard isn't that complicated. Plus, you have plenty of items that can benefit you, with plenty of excesses to start a thriving side business from your home. So, get to work on planning your backyard beekeeping hive.

LAST WORD

In this book, I have tried to cover the basics of starting a backyard beekeeping business and how to start and grow your new business.

After a few initial trials, once you master how to manage bee colonies, it is time for you to develop a solid and precise business plan. No, I am not asking you to write a 20-page business plan but a plan that outlines your process and goals. A plan is one where you figure out which direction you want to go. These are the five things you must decide first:

1. The location and size of your bee colony (I recommend starting small first)
2. What type of bee would populate your colony?
3. What packaging and labeling will you have for your honey
4. Where and how you will market your honey.
5. What pricing should you have for your honey

Remember to start small and scale up your business as your sales grow. Don't invest a lot of money at the beginning in buying a lot of equipment and supplies. Keep your focus on your business's quality and marketing side, and you will see success sooner rather than later.

Hopefully, this book gives you a good general overview of starting a beehive and your own business. Now get out there and start your first colony—and be successful. Remember, we only live once, so why not try to be your best and see where that may take you?

I wanted to thank you for buying my book. I am not a professional writer or author but a person who has always been passionate about growing natural beehives for organic honey. In this book, I wanted to share my knowledge with you, as I know many people share the same passion and drive as I do. So, this book is entirely dedicated to you.

Despite my best efforts to make this book error-free, I want to ask for your forgiveness if you happen to find any errors.

Remember, my writing skills may not be the

best, but the knowledge I share here is pure and honest.

If you thought I added value and shared valuable information that you can use, please post a review on wherever you bought this book. This will mean the world to me. Thank you so much.

Lastly, I wanted to thank my wife, my life partner Debbie, and my daughter June for all their help and support throughout this book. Without them, this book would not have been possible.

If you need to get in touch with me for any reason, please feel free to email me at

Thank you!

Made in United States
Cleveland, OH
01 April 2025

15687504R00105